Meal Prep

The Essential Meal Prep Guide For Beginners – Lose Weight And Save Time With Meal Prepping

Table of Contents:

Introduction 5

Chapter 1 - What Is Meal Prepping? 6

Chapter 2- How To Meal Prep Properly 10

Chapter 3- Successful Rules of Meal Prepping 15

Chapter 4- Tips and Tricks 18

Chapter 5- How to Lose Weight with Meal Prepping 22

Chapter 6- Freezer Meals 27

Chapter 7- Recipes 35

Breakfast Recipes: 36

Peanut Butter and Banana Overnight Oats 36

Kale and Sweet Potato Hash 37

Breakfast Burritos 38

Best Peanut Butter Granola Bars 39

Gluten-Free, Vegan Waffles 40

Quinoa and Pesto Breakfast Bowl 41

Ham, Cauliflower Rice, and Kale Egg Muffins 42

Peanut Butter and Chocolate Oatmeal Cups 43

Breakfast Taco- Vegan Style 44

Eggs Benedict Casserole 45

Apricot Energy Bars 46

Egg, Polenta, and Refried Beans Skillet 47

Indian Baked Potato and Egg 48

Blueberry Lemon Yogurt Breakfast Cake 49

Sea Salt and Dark Chocolate, Almond Banana Oatmeal Bake ... 50

Breakfast Cookie 51

Avocado and Egg Bowl 52

Parfait 53

Blueberry Chia Seed Pudding 54

Banana Pancakes 55

Lunches: 56

Chicken and Rainbow Veggies 56

Sweet Potato and Chicken Bowls 57

Pesto Chicken Pockets 58

Chicken and Cauliflower Rice 59

Fiesta Chicken Bowls.. 60

Chicken Burrito Bowls 61

Chicken and Veggie Bowl... 62

Red Pepper and Quinoa Chili 63

Cashew Chicken and Quinoa 64

No Mayo Tuna Salad 65

Greek Chicken Salad in a Jar... 66

Pasta Salad in a Jar 67

Dinners:... 67

Mushroom Bolognese... 68

Bourbon Peach Butter Grilled Chicken 70

Carrots and Chickpea Couscous 71

Pulled Pork Sandwiches... 72

Pot Roast and Turnip Greens 73

Beef Daube.. 75

Pasta with Meat Sauce 77

Pork Posole 79

Root Vegetable Pot Pie... 80

Chicken and Hominy Verde Stew 82

Chickpea Curried Stew... 84

Lamb Tagine 86

Chapter 8- 28 Day Meal Plan **87**

Week 1... 87

Week 2 89

Week 3 91

Week 4 93

Conclusion **95**

Introduction

Meal prepping is not just the latest craze, it is a great way for anyone that is busy to save time, to save money, and to improve his or her diet. By spending only a few hours a week prepping your meals, you can make huge changes in your life.

This book was created to help you do just that. You are going to learn everything that you need to know about meal prepping. You will learn how to begin prepping your meals, how to store your meals, and how to make sure you are getting the proper nutrition.

You will be provided with tons of delicious recipes that you can make right in your own kitchen in advance so that they are ready for you when you are ready to eat. You are going to learn how by using meal prepping you improve your health and lose weight, how you can become more organized, and how you can reduce the stress in your life.

At the end of this book you will be provided with a 28-day meal plan using the recipes in this book. This book can be used to help get you started meal prepping or to walk you through the entire process. As you work through this book, follow what it says and do not try to rush yourself.

Rushing is only going to make meal prep difficult and just another chore that you do not want to deal with on the long list of chores that you already have. Let meal prepping be fun, get your family involved, or get your friends involved.

If you have a group of friends that wants to meal prep with you, one great way to reduce the food that you have to prep is to have each person prep multiples of the same meals the swap meals once a week.

Most importantly, don't worry about trying to be perfect and do exactly as everyone else does, make meal prepping fit into your life, so that it makes your life easier.

Chapter 1 - What Is Meal Prepping?

We are busy. There is no way around it, but we still need to provide our families with healthy homemade meals. That is why so many people are turning to meal prepping. Meal prepping is going to allow you to eliminate some of the stress from your life by ensuring that you do not have to cook a meal from scratch every single night. Meal prepping also helps you to reduce the amount of time that you are in the kitchen and it can help keep you healthy as well.

You can choose to just meal prep your dinners, or you can do breakfast, lunch, and dinner as well as snacks if you want. The number of meals that you choose to prep is completely up to you and it will all depend on how much time you want to dedicate each week to prepping.

Meal prepping is basically preparing the food that you are going to eat ahead of time so that you can stick to a specific diet or schedule. Cooked foods, as well as raw foods, are included in meal prepping. There are many different ways to use meal prepping and many different benefits as well.

One of the things that hits people the hardest when they are trying to eat healthily or include more home cooked meals is the amount of time that they have to spend cooking, however, meal prepping can reduce this drastically because most of the cooking is done on one day of the week.

Meal prepping is a great way to help you find a bit of balance in your life by taking just a bit of time at the start of the week, you will find that you have a lot more time during the rest of the week to do the things you enjoy.

Why Meal Prep?

People choose to meal prep for many different reasons. Some choose to meal prep because they want to live a healthy lifestyle. They want to have the energy that comes with eating healthy, but because life is so busy they find it hard to take the time each day to make their meals. Meal prepping ensures that they are able to stay consistent which helps them to reach their goals.

Another reason that people choose to meal prep is because they are busy and the idea of coming home after a long day at work just to stand over the stove and cook a meal is overwhelming. It is usually time that determines what they are eating, which leads us to the third reason.

The third reason that many people choose to meal prep is because they are tired of picking food up through the drive thru, ordering out, spending far too much money on food, and putting unhealthy foods into their bodies.

Meal prep simply means meal preparation, which is simply planning your meals, preparing them and packaging them for the upcoming days. Most people that meal prep will prepare meals a week in advance, however, those that use the freezer meal system can prep their meals up to a month in advance.

The great thing about meal prepping is that there is no right or wrong way to do it. You will prep your meals according to what works best for you and your family. The goal of meal prepping is not just to save time in the kitchen, but also to ensure you have access to homemade, healthy meals every day of the week.

Meal prepping is going to:

- ***Help you save money***. Many people believe that eating healthy is more expensive, however, this does not have to be the case, especially if you meal prep. When you meal prep, you are going to buy some of your foods in bulk. This is going to save you a ton of money. On top of that, you are going to know exactly what meals you are going to create which is going to give you a plan when you go to the grocery store. When you walk in with a plan, you are going to know exactly what you need to purchase instead of wandering aimlessly or returning to the store several times during the week to grab extra ingredients. As if that was not enough, when you meal prep your lunches, you are going to cut your cost because you will not be going out to pick up expensive food when you are on your lunch break.

- Meal prepping is going to *help you lose weight*. Knowing what you are going to eat is very important if you want to lose weight. Meal prepping is going to help ensure that you know exactly what is going into your body and it is going to help with portion control. You are going to know in advance how many calories you are eating and you are going to feel more energetic because you are eating healthy foods.

- When you meal prep, you are going to find that *grocery shopping is much easier* for you. Each week, you are going to be able to walk into the grocery store with your list and know exactly what you need to purchase. This is going to reduce impulse buys and help you avoid areas of the store such as the cookie aisle where you are tempted.

- Meal prepping is going to *help you control the portions of the meals that you are eating*. When your meals are already packaged and ready to go, it reduces the chances that you are going to go back and get more.

- *Reducing waste* is a huge benefit of meal prepping. How many times have you had to throw out food because it has gone bad in your fridge? When you meal prep, you are going to make sure that you use up all of your ingredients, each week and if you plan correctly, there are going to be no leftovers to go bad.

- Meal prepping is a huge *time saver*. You will have to spend some time once a week, creating your meal plan and grocery list as well as prepping your meals, but overall, you are going to save a ton of time. Think about how much time you have wasted trying to figure out what you should cook. Think about all of the time, that you spend each night standing in front of the stove or cleaning up after you cook a meal. All of that is done once and all you have to do is heat your food up.

- When you meal prep, you are *investing in your own health*. Because you are going to be choosing what you will eat in advance, it is very likely that you will eat healthier, cleaner meals than people who do not practice meal prepping. Of course, eating healthy will lead to weight loss, but more importantly, it will lead to a healthy body.

- ***Cravings are going to stop*** as you continue to meal prep. In just a few weeks, you will find that you no longer crave sugar or junk. Instead, you will be looking forward to the meals and snacks that you have prepared.

- Stress is a killer. It can cause so many problems with your health such as increasing your blood pressure. It can cause sleep issues, lower your immune system, and even cause digestive problems. Meal planning can ***reduce some of the stress in your life*** and allow you a bit of time to relax each day. It is great to know that when you come home after work, your food is already prepared and ready for you to eat.

- Meal prepping is going to ***ensure that you are eating a variety of foods and that your body is getting the nutrition*** that it needs. You don't have to eat the same meals every single week, mix it up and try out some new recipes.

Chapter 2- How To Meal Prep Properly

Before you begin meal prepping it is important for you to have a lot of storage containers on hand. They should be about the same size and shape so that it is easy for you to stack them and easier for you to find the meals you are looking for.

Many people who choose to start meal prepping decide that they are going to jump in and prep all of their meals, however, it is better if you start small and then make small changes if you want to be successful. Focus on prepping one meal for the entire week. Dinner is usually the best meal to start with. If you are in the habit of skipping breakfast, take a few minutes each night and prep for your breakfast the next morning, creating overnight oats or boiling a few eggs.

Once you have collected your storage containers and you have decided what meals you are going to prep, you will want to take a look at your schedule and decide which day is going to work best for you to do your meal prepping.

Some people do their meal prepping on Sundays other people choose to use Monday, I personally do my meal prep on Thursdays because that is the day that I go shopping and the kids are at school so I am not interrupted. This allows me to dedicate the entire day to shopping, meal prep, and taking care of other chores that need to be done. It really is best if you do your grocery shopping on the same day that you plan on doing your meal prep.

When planning your meals, you want to keep them simple. It is very tempting to start creating very complicated dishes because you are preparing them in advance, however, when you are first starting out, it is much better to keep things as simple as possible. Boiling a dozen eggs is a very easy way for you to add some protein to your breakfast, cooking a chicken is going to allow you to have shredded chicken all week to add to your lunches, or cooking a big batch of rice will ensure you have the whole grains you need. Once you get into the routine of prepping your meals, you can make them more complex.

Meal prepping can be done for any lifestyle. If you want vegan meals, you can prep them very easily, vegetarian and meat based meals are just as easy to prep.

Once you have chosen the day that you will do your shopping and prep your meals, it is time for you to start planning out the meals that you are going to make.

Each meal should include a vegetable, protein (vegans can get this from vegetables), a starch, healthy fat, and a fruit if desired.

Begin by writing down all of your options for each type of food. For example, if you are going to include protein in each of your meals, write down all of the sources of protein that you can use in your meals. Put a star next to your favorite sources of protein. Do this for each type of food. A few examples of plant based proteins are beans, tofu, edamame, and tempeh.

Plan all of your meals based off of your list of foods. Once the meals are planned, write down all of the ingredients that you will need to purchase.

After your shopping trip, you are ready to start meal prepping. You will want to cook all of the proteins using a variety of different spices and seasonings. Don't forget about your crockpot. Using your crockpot can make meal prep so much easier and it is great for large batches of shredded chicken.

When you are purchasing your meat, you want to make sure that it is already thawed because purchasing frozen meat can really throw your meal prep off.

Remember, there are different levels of prepping. A meal prepper that is just starting out will generally prep one meal for the entire week. Someone who has been meal prepping for a while may prep all of his or her dinners, lunches and maybe even a few lunches or snacks. The advanced meal prepper will prep all of their meals, snacks and may even create a few freezer meals, which we will talk about later in this book.

However, do not let the determine how you meal prep. You should always focus on prepping in a way that works best for you and your family. If cooking all of the food one day is far too much for you to handle, split it up between a couple of days.

How To Create A Meal Prep Schedule

The first thing that you need to think about when you are creating your meal prep schedule is the type of foods that you are going to be prepping. If you eat a meat based diet, you will be spending a large amount of your time preparing meat. If you eat a vegetarian or vegan diet, you will be spending a lot of your time, peeling and chopping vegetables.

The next step is to pick your meal prep day or days. You can split your meal prep up, for example, spend your morning prepping your vegetables while your meat thaws. Then after you have enjoyed your afternoon, spend the evening prepping your meat. Perhaps you want to prep your meat one evening and your vegetables and other foods the next. Whatever works best for you is what you want to do.

Don't forget, you can accomplish other chores while you are meal prepping. For example, challenge yourself to chop all of your vegetables before you need to switch the next load of laundry. Wash the dishes or deep clean the kitchen while the meat is cooking or the vegetables are roasting.

You can also sneak a bit of prepping in throughout the week to help reduce the amount of time you spend in the kitchen on your prep days. For example, if you have five minutes, you can prep your lunch for the following day or prep some fruit for your smoothie in the morning.

Create some overnight oats for breakfast the next morning when you have a few minutes, scramble some eggs to reheat the next morning, or toss some chicken in the crockpot to cook and be shredded later.

It is important to remember that everyone's life is different. We all have different schedules and we are all going to prep our meals differently. The guidelines that are in this book are simply here to help you make meal prep work for you in your life.

Preparing For A Day Of Meal Prepping

Step 1- Take inventory

The first thing that you want to do when you are preparing for your day of meal prepping is to take inventory of what you already have in your cabinets, freezer, and refrigerator.

Create a list of all of the items that you have. As you are going through the recipes that you plan on cooking check your list to determine if you already have any of the ingredients. Make sure that you put a check mark next to them if you are going to use them in a recipe so that you do not plan on using the same ingredient more than once. This is not only going to save you money and time, but it is also going to help you use up the foods that are taking up space in your kitchen.

Step 2- Organize

While you are taking inventory, you will want to organize. Clean out your cabinets, wipe them down and put all of the food back in them, making sure that they are organized. Do the same to your fridge, freezer and deep freeze.

It is very important that you clean out your refrigerator because, with all of the food that you are going to prep, you are going to want to make sure that you have space in your fridge. Make sure that when you put the prepped foods in the fridge, the foods that you are going to eat first are in the front.

Step 3- Put It On The Calendar

So many times, I have seen people create these meal plans, make wonderful grocery lists, buy all of the ingredients that they need, then by Tuesday, they have no idea what they are supposed to cook. In order to avoid this, put your meals on your calendar. You can purchase a calendar for your kitchen that is used specifically for your meal plan.

This way, when it comes time to grab your prepped food out of the fridge, all you have to do is look at your calendar and you will know exactly what you need to grab. When you are adding the meals to your calendar, make sure that you check your schedule. There is no reason to prep lunch on Thursday if there is going to be a team lunch at work. There is no reason to prep dinner if you know you are going to be visiting family one evening for dinner. Making sure that you are not over prepping is going to make things a lot easier for you.

Step 4- Schedule it

There is no point in doing all of the preparation when it comes to meal prepping if you don't have the time to actually prep the meals. Make sure that you have time scheduled each week for your meal prepping, even if you have to split it up over a few evenings.

Chapter 3- Successful Rules of Meal Prepping

Meal prepping can save a lot of time as well as a lot of money, which is going to help reduce the stress in your life. While it can seem overwhelming at first, once you get started you will find that you never want to go back to cooking your meals every day but instead, prefer meal prepping. In order to ensure your success, I want to provide you with rules that you can follow to help you incorporate meal prepping into your life.

1. ***Split up your tasks throughout the week.*** Choose one night of the week to clean and organize your kitchen, taking inventory of the ingredients that you already have. Choose another night to search for healthy, simple recipes that you can prepare ahead of time. On another night, create your grocery list and add your meals to your calendar. Prep your veggies and carbs one night, then your protein on another night. Do whatever you have to do to make sure you can fit everything that needs to be done into your schedule.

2. ***Map out your shopping trip.*** While it is great for you to create a grocery list, it is better for you to know exactly where you are going to get the food. You can start out by grabbing the flyers to the stores that you frequently shop at. Create a list for each store that you will be going to in order to ensure that no ingredients are forgotten. Then clip your coupons. Finally, know where the foods that you are going to purchase are found in each store that you will be stopping at. For example, if you need quinoa, know where this is located and at what store you will be purchasing it. This reduces the amount of time that you have to spend wandering the aisles and it reduces the chances of you making impulse buys.

3. ***Make sure that you have enough storage containers.*** It is very easy to overestimate the number of storage containers that you have. Make sure that each of your containers have lids as well. If you do not have enough make sure that you pick more up before you begin your meal prep. You can also use plastic freezer bags for certain meals as well.

4. ***Prep your meals on a day when you will not be rushed.*** Our lives are stressful and busy enough, there is no reason for you to constantly feel rushed, especially when you are prepping your meals. Instead, choose a day when you can relax and enjoy the process of prepping your meals. For example, on my meal prep

day, I get up in the morning just like any other day, pick up the house, get the kids ready for school, send them off, then go for a jog. After my jog, I head out to the grocery stores. When I get home, I lay all of the food out, grab my list and recipes, turn on some music, and start prepping. By the time the kids get home from school, I am done and we can go on with our normal evening.

You may be sitting there thinking, oh yes, that sounds so easy, but I work 40 hours a week. Don't worry, so do I and generally many more hours than that, when you follow the guidelines in this book, you will find that you are able to make the time. If, however, you do not feel that you can please, sit down and take a look at your schedule. No one should ever be so busy that they don't even have the time to prepare their meals.

5. Before you begin meal prepping *it is important for you to learn a little bit about the foods that you are going to be eating*. You want to be able to make sure that you are eating a balanced diet and that you are getting enough calories in your diet.

6. When you are planning the meals that you are going to be eating for the week, *try to choose recipes that contain some of the same ingredients.* For example, if you are creating a dish on Monday that needs rice, try to find a dish that you can make later in the week that uses rice as well or look for recipes that will allow you to use your leftover rice in them.

7. If you can't stand the idea of eating the same type of food two days in a row, don't worry about it. *Create two or three side dishes for the entire week* and alternate them in the meals that you are creating.

8. *Consider choosing recipes that you can freeze.* Not all foods are going to stay good in the fridge for an entire week. That is why it is really good to choose a few freezer meals each week when you are determining what recipes you will prep. Chili, soups, stews, and many other meals are great for prepping ahead of time and freezing. I will talk more about freezer meals a bit later in this book.

9. *Keep it raw if you need to.* It is very easy to prep recipes such as enchiladas or casseroles, however, sometimes these do not taste the best if they have been reheated. If you do not want to spend the time making the meal on the night you want to eat it, but want it to be fresh, simply prepare the recipe and do not cook it.

Instead, prepare it in the baking dish, cover it and place it in the freezer, then all you have to do is pop it in the oven when you are ready to eat it.

10. **Label everything.** It does not matter if you are creating freezer meals or prepping food to keep in your fridge, make sure that you are labeling every container. You can use dry erase markers on your plastic storage containers or sharpies on your freezer bags. Make sure that you write down the date that the meal was prepped, the night that you plan on eating it, how many servings are in the container, and what is in the container. You do not want to expect to pull out a baking pan of enchiladas and end up with lasagna.

Chapter 4- Tips and Tricks

It does not matter why you choose to prep your meals, if you are super busy and don't have time to cook during the week, if you are tired of eating convenience food, or if you are trying to get healthy, the tips in this chapter are going to make food prep much easier for you.

What is great about these tips is that they are going to work for you whether you are prepping your food just for you or for your entire family. What many people love about meal prep is that there is a huge community of people online that are sharing all of the recipes that they use so there is no shortage of options. The tips in this chapter are from the meal prep pros, and are guaranteed to make your meal prep faster, easier, and more successful.

1. ***Keep staples on hand.*** Even if you are not prepping all of your meals, it is best to keep staples such as tempeh, boiled eggs, oatmeal, bananas, baked sweet potatoes, and shredded chicken on hand. When you keep staples like this on hand, you are going to be able to quickly create meals so that you do not end up grabbing convenience foods.

2. ***Make sure that your containers of functional.*** Your containers are going to determine how successful you are at meal prepping. You want to make sure that your containers are going to protect your food and keep it fresh until you are ready to eat it, that they can be stacked easily, they are microwave and dishwasher safe and that they are the right size. You do not want to use huge containers to hold small amounts of food because they will take up precious space in your fridge.

3. ***Don't feel like you have to go on Pinterest and create the most complicated meals*** because this is only going to lead to a bunch of Pinterest fails. Instead, use fruits and veggies that are in season, create simple recipes such as overnight oatmeal that do not take a lot of time or work to prepare. When your recipes are simple, you can add the spices that you want to them as well as other ingredients. Imagine creating a pot of simple chili one night and then adding a few extra spices and serving it over spaghetti the next night. It is great when you can create two meals out of one.

4. ***Practice makes perfect*** when it comes to many things in life including meal prepping. Start off simple by prepping your veggies, putting them in one container, your proteins in another container, and your carbs in a third container. This will allow you to create amazing meals in no time flat. While the meals are not going to be completely prepared, you are going to be reducing the amount of time that you are spending preparing them each evening. As you get better at meal prep, you can create entire meals.

5. ***Get to know your vegetables.*** Not all vegetables are going to keep in the fridge for one week after they have been chopped. Freezing certain vegetables is going to change their texture and their taste. Vegetables that have a high-water content are not going to last more than a couple of days in the fridge after they have been chopped. If you are slicing or chopping vegetables into sticks, you can store them in water in your fridge to keep them fresh and crunchy.

6. ***Make sure that you plan your snacks and never leave the house without your water, snack, and meal*** if you are going to be gone for long. This is going to reduce your chances of hitting the drive thru, ensuring that you are eating the foods that you have prepped.

7. ***Make prepping a party.*** Meal prep does take time, however, it is not a waste of time and should never be seen that way. You can multitask while you are meal prepping or you can make meal prepping fun. Have a friend come over to help with meal prepping, or listen to music, do some exercises while you are stirring the vegetables, or get some of your chores done around the house as your meals cook.

8. ***Cook all of the same foods at once.*** One of the great things about meal prepping is that you can cook once and create several meals. For example, if you are making tacos and sloppy joes this week, you can cook all of the ground beef at the same time and then separate it into different meals after it cooks. Cook all of your chicken at the same time and then separate it creating different meals with different ingredients. For example, I will cook a huge amount of chicken breasts in my crockpots. After they have cooked I will shred them. I will add some to the filling of my enchiladas, some will go into my salads, and some will go into my chicken tacos. I have cooked once and created several meals.

9. ***Purchase containers that are of proper proportion.*** If you are creating 7 dinners for a family of 4, make sure that your containers are only going to hold 4 servings. If you are prepping lunches for yourself, make sure that your containers

will only hold 1 serving. This is going to ensure that you are not overeating and that no foods are going to waste.

10. After prepping all of your meals, no one wants to spend even more time cleaning up. In order to **reduce your clean up time**, take a few steps while you are prepping your food to do so. For example, line your baking dishes with aluminum foil. This is great if you know you will be using the same baking dish several times and it is great to reduce the amount of scrubbing you have to do. Wash your pots and pans as you finish using them instead of waiting until you have finished all of the meal prep to do so. When you finish cooking one food, wash the pan while the other foods continue to cook. By the time you are finished prepping all of your foods, you will not have any dishes left to wash.

    You can also clean as you go. If you spill something on the stove, wipe it up instead of letting it dry on and struggling to get it off later. Wash your knives, blender, chopping boards, and food processor as you go. Do whatever you need to make sure that the mess is not piling up around you. This will ensure that when you are done with your meal prep, you can walk out of the kitchen and it will still be clean.

11. **Purchase bags of frozen produce when possible.** A lot of times you are going to find that frozen produce is cheaper than fresh, however, they taste the same and they are going to provide you with the same nutrition. The great thing about frozen produce is that you can pop the leftovers back in the freezer and not have to worry about it going bad before you cook again. Fresh produce has to be eaten quickly and can make it difficult to prep an entire weeks' worth of meals.

12. **Make more than you will eat and then freeze the extra.** This is going to apply to cooked foods much more than it will raw fruits and vegetables, however, it is a great way to cut down on your meal prep time each week. When I make a soup, I do not make enough soup for one night, but instead, I make enough for 4 nights. This way, I can put it in a freezer bag, freeze it and have it 4 more nights throughout the rest of the month. You can freeze beans, rice, quinoa, as well as all different types of dinners.

13. When you are first starting out, **choose your trigger meal to prep.** Your trigger meal is going to be the meal that you are most likely to turn to prepackaged or fast food to get When you start by prepping your trigger meal, you are going to be cutting the junk out and making sure that your body is getting the nutrients that it needs.

14. If you are prepping all of your meals don't forget to give yourself some variety. It is very easy to get tired of eating the same thing every single day or even every week. Try a few different recipes every now and then.

15. **Cook multiple foods at the same time.** There is no reason that you cannot bake chicken and roast your vegetables in your oven at the same time. This is a great way for you to reduce the amount of time that you are spending in your kitchen.

16. **Once you have cooked all of your rice or quinoa, make sure that you use all of it.** Your body needs whole grains, it needs carbohydrates in order to provide you with the energy that you need. There are plenty of ways that you can use your rice or quinoa and in the process, you will be ensuring that your body gets all of the nutrients that it needs.

There are so many ways for you to ensure your success as you are meal prepping, but the best tip that I can give you is to just keep at it. The more you meal prep the better you will become at it and the more you will enjoy it.

Meal prepping is not supposed to feel like a burden or another task that you have to complete, but instead, it is supposed to help you simplify your life while saving time and energy.

Chapter 5- How to Lose Weight with Meal Prepping

We spend hours each week planning out our schedules if we are going to go on a trip, we make sure that everything is planned and perfect, yet when it comes to our diets, we just grab whatever is convenient.

If we want to live a healthy life and we want to lose weight, we need to be dedicated to ensuring that we are providing our bodies with the fuel that it needs. Meal prepping can help us do that. The reason that many people are overweight is because they just don't have the time to create healthy home cooked meals, or they think they don't have the time.

Our schedules are packed, it is almost a miracle if we actually get 6 to 8 hours of sleep let alone create homemade healthy meals. However, being busy does not have to stop you from losing weight, feeling great about your body, and improving your health.

Meal prepping ensures that even if you have a hectic week at work if you get sick if some unforeseen circumstance arises or whatever, happens, you can still stick to your plan and eat healthy foods instead of turning to junk.

If you want to use meal prepping to help you lose weight, there are a few steps that you have to take. Throughout this book, I have talked about healthy meals. However, it is very simple to create unhealthy meals when you are meal prepping as well. This means that in order for you to ensure that your body is getting all of the nutrients that it needs, you need to make sure that you are creating healthy dishes, prepping healthy meals, and then actually eating them.

Breakfast is vital if you want to lose weight, however, it is a meal that so many of us skip or we just grab a cup of coffee as we run out of the door. Of course, there is always the option of swinging by the drive thru in order to grab some greasy calorie packed sandwich that we scarf down on the way to work.

Instead, simply take the time to prep your breakfast. There are so many options and even if you do create a breakfast sandwich, it is going to be much better for you than anything that you would purchase from a drive thru.

It is vital that you pay attention to the calories that you are consuming. I know, I know, but I am eating healthy foods, why do I have to count calories? The fact is that eating too much of any food, even healthy foods will make you gain weight. Let's think about it for a moment. Imagine that you wake up in the morning and you drink a huge green smoothie that contains 800 calories. Then you eat a salad for lunch that contains another 800 calories. Before you factor in any snacks or dinner, you have already gone over your daily calorie allowance.

While those foods are going to provide your body with more vitamins and minerals than a few double cheeseburgers, calories are still calories. A great way to find out how many calories that you need each day is the free app called my fitness pal or you can visit the website. However, you determine how many calories you need in a day, you will also need to know how to break those calories down per meal.

Let's look at a 1500 calorie diet. If you are supposed to eat 1500 calories per day and you are eating three meals plus two snacks, you need to be able to break your calories up so that you are getting enough throughout the day.

First, you will divide the number of calories that you eat each day by 4. This is 375 if you are eating a 1500 calorie a day diet. Therefore, your breakfast, lunch, and dinner should all be about 375 calories each. Then you will take the left over 375 calories and divide that by 2 which is 187.5 and that is the number of calories your snacks can have in them.

The next thing that you need to spend some time thinking about is your food struggles. Perhaps you are one of those people that have a hard time eating breakfast before you leave the house in the mornings. You will need to acknowledge this struggle and then be honest with yourself about what you will actually eat. You see, if you choose a food that you are not going to eat in the morning you are no better off. If you are in a hurry in the morning, choose a healthy breakfast burrito or take a smoothie with you when you head to work.

If lunch is a struggle for you then you will want to focus on prepping a healthy lunch option that you can grab on your way to work in the mornings. If that 3 pm lull seems to be when you are most tempted to eat junk, make sure that you pack a simple snack as well.

Dinners can be extremely difficult. Coming home after a long day at work, dealing with homework, chores, bills, emails, the phone ringing off of the hook, and in the midst of it, you are supposed to make dinner. It is no wonder so many people turn to easy, prepackaged foods, however, these foods are not going to provide your body with the nutrients that it needs. If preparing a healthy dinner is one of your food struggles, that is where you will want to focus when you first begin meal prepping.

Of course, food, in general, could be the struggle. It is very easy to get caught up in this life and feel like you don't have time to worry about or deal with food. This leads to meals that consist of nothing more than coffee or a can of soda. Eventually, you will become so hungry that you eat everything in sight and doing this over and over will lead to weight gain. If you struggle with getting enough food, you may want to prep 2 or 3 days' worth of meals and snacks at a time because you will need to prep all of your meals and snacks.

You want to create some snack, grab bags. One of the biggest calorie busters of most people's diet is grabbing a family sized container of nuts, chips, or crackers. Before you know it, the container is empty and you don't even remember eating the food. Instead of allowing yourself to do this. Purchase some snack sized storage bags. Place one portion of the food in the storage bags and grab one when you need a snack. This will not only ensure that you are not eating the entire container, but it is also going to ensure that you have a quick snack to grab and take with you when you are in a hurry.

If you want to change your diet and begin eating healthy, but you don't want to be limited to eating recipes that you have made in advance, simply keep your fridge and freezer stocked with healthy basics. Prepared quinoa, rice, chicken, fruit, salad, and oatmeal are great staples to keep in your fridge so that you can quickly prepare a meal out of ingredients that have already been prepped.

Personally, I find that this works great, however, I prefer to know that the entire meal is already prepped and ready to go. I love knowing that for the week or for however long I have prepped my meals for, I don't have to even think about what I am going to eat. It is already taken care of and ready for me to grab.

When you are prepping your meals, you will do so according to your own needs. When you meal prep, you are creating structure for your diet and the amount of structure that you need to create depends on your lifestyle.

You may find that you just need a little help in the mornings and that prepping breakfast is all that you need or you may find that you need a bit more structure. However, much you need to prep is completely up to you. Don't allow the amount of time that you have to discourage you. If you only have an hour to focus on meal prep today, do everything that you can within that hour. Then spend more time on it another day. When you continue to do this, you will find that more of your time is free and even better, you will start losing weight and feeling healthy.

Meal Prep Mistakes That Can Cause Weight Gain

Meal prepping can be great for your health and it can be great for your waistline as well, however, if it is not done properly it can actually cause you to gain weight. There are a few common mistakes that can derail your weight loss journey while you are meal prepping that you want to make sure you avoid.

1. ***Prepping too much food*** can definitely cause you to gain weight. When you prep too much food, you have more food than you need for your meals and if you don't realize that you have prepped too much, it can end up in your storage containers. This will cause you to eat too many calories and as we already discussed, too many calories, no matter what food they come from will make you gain weight.

   In order to ensure that you are prepping the right amount of food, all you have to do is to use some measuring cups. If one serving of brown rice is ½ of a cup, and you are going to be creating 5 meals with rice, you know that you will need 2.5 cups of brown rice. If you make any more than that, you are going to be eating too much.

   On top of this, if you are prepping too much food and not eating it, then it is going to waste. The food that you prep is only going to stay good in your fridge for about 5 days. After 5 days, you are either going to have to toss the leftovers or freeze them.

2. On the opposite side of the spectrum, you may ***not be prepping enough food.*** If you are trying to reduce your portions too dramatically or are very afraid of going over your portions, you may not prep enough food. This can get very annoying because you are going to be stuck eating very small portions. If your portions are not large enough, this could lead to snacking and if it does not, it will still lead to weight gain. If you do not eat enough, your body is going to hold on to everything that you do eat because it is going to be afraid that there is not enough food.

   There is no perfect way to solve these two issues except for making sure that you check the portion sizes and make sure that you are getting enough calories in each of your meals. When you first start prepping your meals, you will want to pay attention to how you feel. If you are still hungry after you have eaten, you will want to make a note of that and increase your portion sizes.

3. Another huge mistake that many people make when they begin prepping their meals is that they ***purchase sauces and dressings from the grocery store.***

Salads and dressings that you purchase at the grocery store are packed with sugar, sodium, and calories. It is very easy to make your own homemade sauces, or it is even better if you add flavor to your meals by using herbs and spices. Olive oil or lemon juice can also be used to add a bit of flavor to your meals.

4. Finally, the last mistake that many people make when they are prepping their meals is that they ***make food that they do not like.*** A lot of people will prep foods just because they know the foods are good for them, but they never take into consideration if they will actually eat the foods. If you don't like a specific food, choose a different food. For example, I do not eat meat, therefore, instead of prepping chicken, I will prep tofu. I hate asparagus, which means there is no point in me prepping it so instead I prep other vegetables.

There is no reason for you to waste your time or your money on foods that you are not going to eat. Don't force yourself to eat certain foods because they are supposed to be good for you, but instead eat foods because you like the way that they taste. This is not to say that you should never try new foods, but if you find that you do not like them, don't make yourself eat them.

Chapter 6- Freezer Meals

When things get really busy and you are struggling to prepare your meals, freezer meals can help. You can make freezer meals part of your weekly meal prepping or you can make them up to a month in advance. They are wonderful for ensuring that you have delicious homemade meals ready to go on those nights when you just don't have time to cook or just don't feel like it and they are a great way to make sure you stick to your diet.

Bulk cooking is something that many people have started doing in their lives in order to reduce the amount of time that they spend in the kitchen after a long day at work. Creating freezer meals does take some time, however, it is entirely possible to create healthy freezer meals that you can have for dinner every night while prepping your fresh breakfasts, lunches, and snacks.

Freezer meals have many benefits, including saving money on those expensive takeout meals when you just don't feel like cooking, but it is going to give you more freedom from being chained to your kitchen every night. Pulling a bag out of the freezer and dumping it in the crockpot before you leave for work, or grabbing a casserole out of the freezer when you get home will give you time to focus on more important things. Of course, this is also going to help ensure that your kitchen stays cleaner as well.

Freezer meals are going to allow you to enjoy some down time, they can be taken with you when you go on vacation, and you always know exactly what is in the food that you are preparing so if there are any allergies in the family, you don't have to worry.

What Can Be Frozen?

You can freeze stews, casseroles, soups, pasta sauces, chicken, burritos, chili, and so many other meals. This means that you don't just have to eat foods that can be made in a crockpot every night. It is very easy to bag up vegetables for fajitas or stir fries, and you can even create meal kits.

Desserts from the freezer are wonderful as well. There is nothing better than being able to pull out a fresh apple pie and bake it whenever the urge hits. You can stock up on healthy fruits when they are in season and at their lowest price then create amazing desserts with them.

How Does It Work?

Freezer meals are prepared ahead of time, which makes them a great addition to your meal prep routine. You can create freezer meals a few different ways. You can make them on the day that you work on your meal prep and make a week to a month's worth of freezer meals. Or the other option is to simply double or even quadruple your meals as you cook them and then place the extra servings in your freezer. What you choose will depend completely upon how much time you have to spare and how many meals you want to create.

What is really great about freezer meals is that you are able to purchase all of the items that you need in one shopping trip which is going to save you a ton of money as well as a ton of time, especially if you create freezer meals for the entire month.

Freezer Meal Tips

1. ***Make sure that you schedule enough time.*** It is going to take about 1 hour to make 16 freezer meals. This will usually be 4 recipes made 4 times. Therefore, if you want to make an entire months' worth of freezer meals, you will want to make sure you plan for about 2 hours of cooking.

2. To reduce the amount of time that you are spending on your freezer meals, you can ***keep chopped vegetables*** such as onions or peppers as well as cooked meat and cheese on hand.

3. If you want to reduce the amount that you are spending on groceries, make sure that you ***stock up on soups, canned tomatoes, meats, sauces, and beans*** when they are on sale.

4. Make sure that you are ***using a freezer bag that is of high quality.*** You do not want to purchase the cheapest freezer bags possible when you are making freezer meals because you want your foods to be protected.

5. When you freeze your meals, ***lay the bag on the side so that it flattens out***, after the meals are frozen, you can move them to create more space.

6. ***Thaw your freezer meals out in a large bowl in your fridge*** in order to ensure the bags do not leak. Freezer bags can get holes in them and they will at some point. Putting the freezer bag in a bowl to thaw ensures not only that you do not have a huge mess in your fridge, but that you do not lose any of your food as well.

7. When you are creating freezer meals, ***use freezer bags instead of storage containers.*** Not only is this going to take up less space, but it is going to ensure that there is less for you to clean up.

8. ***Place your freezer bags in a storage container*** when you are filling them up to prevent them from spilling.

9. When you are creating multiples of the same recipe, ***line the bags up and measure out each of the ingredients into the bags once.*** For example, place all of the onions into each of the freezer bags when creating chili, followed by all of the canned tomatoes and so on.

10. Always ***make sure that you are labeling all of the freezer bags*** with the recipe that they contain, cooking directions, as well as the date that they were made.

11. ***Start out using recipes that are specifically for freezer meals.*** You will find some of these at the end of this book. Recipes that are written for freezer meals are going to walk you through the process step by step.

12. ***Always make sure that you are planning out the freezer meal process.*** You will need to plan time to decide what meals you are going to make, to plan your shopping trips and your prepping days. You want to make sure that you know what stores you will be going to, what coupons you will be using if any, and even what order you will visit the stores in. The better planned the day, the more successful you are going to be.

13. ***Choose a variety of meals that are going to require very little prep work and that have overlapping ingredients.*** Choosing recipes with overlapping ingredients is going to reduce your amount of prep time.

14. ***Always make one batch of a recipe and try it before making it in bulk.*** You do not want to end up with several meals that you do not like or no one will eat.

15. **Do as much of the prep work as you can at the same time.** For example, I begin by prepping all of my vegetables, then I focus on cooking all of the meats. While the meats cook, I open all of the cans of tomatoes, sauces, and so on then pour them into my bags. By the time that the meat is done and cooled, all I have to do is put it in the bags and zip them up.

16. Freezer meals will keep for up to 3 months, so **it is important for you to keep the freezer organized** and keep a running list of what meals you have prepared. This will ensure nothing goes to waste and you know what your options are when you want to use them.

17. **Make sure that you let the freezer meal cool to room temperature** before you freeze it. This usually only takes about 30 minutes.

18. **Remove as much of the air from the freezer bags as you can** before you freeze them. If you are preparing foods in a baking dish, cover them with plastic wrap and then foil in order to keep the air out and ensure they do not get freezer burnt.

19. *Muffins and breads freeze really well.* You will want to **wrap each muffin or slice of bread individually**, which will also help with portion control.

20. If you want to freeze individual portions for smaller meals such as lunch, you can **use silicone muffin tins**. Simply freeze the soup, stew or other food in the muffin tin and then pop them out and place them all in a freezer bag. When you are ready to eat, just pull out one serving.

Foods That Do Not Freeze Well

1. ***Potatoes.*** When you freeze potatoes, it changes the texture as well as the taste. While freezing them will prevent them from spoiling, it is likely that you are not going to want to eat them after they have thawed. However, mashed potatoes are fine for freezing.

2. ***Vegetables and fruits that have a high water content or are delicate*** such as watermelon, citrus fruit, tomatoes, and cucumbers. It is possible for you to freeze some of these foods, for example, tomatoes, if they are going to be cooked but do not expect them to come out of the freezer the same way that you put them in.

3. ***Any sauce or gravy that you have used cornstarch to thicken*** is not going to freeze well because they tend to separate as well as break down in the freezer. Instead of freezing the gravy, simply freeze the stock, and then add the cornstarch after it has been reheated.

4. ***Egg whites*** will become rubbery if you freeze them as will celery. If you are freezing a recipe that contains either, make sure that you chop them finely before freezing.

5. ***Mayonnaise*** is going to break down if it is put in the freezer. If you are freezing a recipe that needs mayonnaise, leave the mayonnaise out and add it in last, when you are ready to cook it.

6. If you are making cakes for desserts, you will want to make sure that you are using a butter cream frosting on them. Other ***frostings*** do not freeze well.

7. ***Pastas*** tend to become too soft if they are frozen and reheated. Personally, I prefer to cook the pasta fresh, 8 to 12 minutes of boiling pasta in order to have a delicious dinner is fine with me. If you want to do it this way, simply add all of the ingredients into your freezer bag except the pasta, then cook the pasta when you are ready to eat the meal. If you want the pasta pre-cooked, under-cook the pasta before putting it in your freezer bag.

8. Cheeses are fine to freeze; however, ***yogurt and sour cream*** will separate when you freeze them.

Preparing for Freezer Meal Prep

Once you decide that you are going to use freezer meals as part of your meal prep routine, you will probably find yourself wondering exactly how you can do it. While having a freezer full of meals that are ready to do is wonderful and makes your life a lot easier, it can seem a bit overwhelming at first. However, if you follow these directions, it does not have to be.

1. ***Take inventory of what you already have.*** This is one thing that so many people forget to do before they start planning their meals which leads to being overrun with cans of tomatoes or beans. While having extra food on hand is not a bad thing, if saving money is a priority, there is no reason for you to not use up the food that you have.

   The idea is to not have much of anything left in your cabinets after your meal prep is done except for some baking staples, spices, grains, and maybe some pasta. Make a list of everything that you have in your cabinets as well as your fridge and start thinking about how you can use that food up. Perhaps you have a few squash left in the fridge and a bag of sweet potatoes. You can easily roast these and toss them in with your lunch. If you have beans in your cabinet, consider making a chili or four and freezing them to eat later.

2. ***Check your sales fliers.*** Let's face it, no matter how much money we have, no one wants to overspend on groceries when we know we could use the money elsewhere. This means that before you start planning those freezer meals, you will want to grab the sales flyers from the stores that you shop at (or look them up online) and figure out what is on sale and how you can use it. For example, if you find chicken on sale for 99 cents a pound, try to plan a lot of your meals around that sale.

3. ***Think about your needs.*** Do you need easy meals that are not going to take a long time to prep or can you devote your entire day to meal prep? Maybe you want to prep simple breakfasts and lunches but want more complex dinners. However, you choose to create your meals you need to do so with your needs in mind. You do not want to choose a bunch of crockpot freezer meals if you know the food is not going to make it into the crockpot in the mornings.

4. The next step is to **_start making a list of all of the ingredients that you are going to need._** Divide your list according to what store you will purchase the items at and what aisle if possible. For example, I will purchase my produce and almond milk at one store, then my tofu and a few other items are purchased at another store, and I even go to a third store. If I did not separate my list into what specific store I was going to get each item, my shopping day could become very stressful and I could forget to purchase a lot of my ingredients.

    Go through your list twice to make sure that you have included everything that you need. I find it easiest if I create a list with every ingredient that I need. I will start with my recipes and write down what I need, doubling or tripling depending on how many freezer meals I plan on making. After I have a list of every ingredient, I will condense it down, for example, if I need 3 bags of brown rice for one recipe and 2 for another, I just add them together and write down 5 bags of brown rice. As I am doing this, I will have three sheets of paper.

    Each sheet of paper is going to be for one specific store. As I go through the ingredients, I will write what I need down on the paper for the store that I plan on purchasing it at. Then, I will go through the list a second time making sure that you have not forgotten to add anything to your list.

5. After you have created your list, it is time for you to go shopping. There are times that just thinking about shopping can wear a person out but if this happens, just **_remind yourself that when you are done prepping your meals, you and your family are going to eat better for the entire month._**

    When you go shopping, try to go alone, if you take your children you could become distracted and you could end up purchasing items that you do not really need. It is a terrible thing when you have all of your food cooking and suddenly you realize that you did not purchase an item that was on your list because you were distracted.

6. Finally, after you have done your shopping it is time for you to **_prep your meals._**

    When you are first starting out, I would suggest that you only focus on one week's worth of food. It is very easy for you to prep your breakfast, lunch, and snacks using the method discussed about in previous chapters, and it is very easy to create a week's worth of dinners using freezer meals.

It is likely that while you are creating your week's worth of freezer meals, you will realize how simple it would be to create multiple meals and eventually you will be able to do this.

When you make a month's worth of freezer meals, not only are you going to free up a ton of your time in the evenings, but you are also going to reduce the amount of time that you spend prepping your meals each week because you will only have to worry about breakfast, lunch, and snacks.

Freezer Meal Benefits

1. Making large batches of food and separating them out into freezer bags to use over a long period of time is going to **save you time, money, and energy.** When you know that you have meals that are ready to eat right at your fingertips, you are going to be less tempted to go out to eat, cleaning up after dinner is going to be a breeze and you can create freezer meals in the same time that it would take to make one meal.

2. You are able to **cook once and eat many times.** When I make my freezer meals, I will make four of each of the seven dinners, which means that I can cook once and eat for an entire month.

3. You are able to **enjoy healthy home-cooked meals with minimal stress.** Of course, prep day can be a bit stressful for anyone, however, if you plan it out properly and allow yourself plenty of time for your planning and prepping it does not have to be stressful at all. In fact, meal prepping can be one of the most relaxing times of your week.

4. One of the things that most people love about having freezer meals is that they **always know what they are going to have for dinner.** They do not find themselves sitting at their desk 30 minutes before it is time to go home wondering what they are going to cook. Nor do they find themselves standing in front of a fridge looking at the food that they have but still unable to come up with any ideas.

Freezer meals and meal prepping help to reduce the stress in your life as well as the anxiety. It saves you time as well as money and it ensures that you will always know what is going into the food that you are eating and when you come home from work at night, you are going to be able to relax instead of standing over a stove and cooking for an hour then cleaning up.

Chapter 7- Recipes

Now that you know everything you need to about meal prepping, you may be trying to figure out how it will work for you. Well, I am going to help you with that. In this chapter, we are going to go over tons of recipes for all of your meals that can be prepped ahead of time in order to not only save you time but money as well.

Breakfast Recipes:

Peanut Butter and Banana Overnight Oats

Ingredients:
- ½ of a banana mashed
- 2 tablespoons of creamy peanut butter
- ¼ of a cup of plain Greek yogurt
- ¾ of a cup of unsweetened almond milk
- 1 tablespoon of honey
- 1 teaspoon of vanilla extract
- 1 cup of rolled oats
- 1 tablespoon of Chia seeds
- 1 teaspoon of ground cinnamon

Method:
1. Begin by mashing ½ of a banana in a large bowl, then add in the peanut butter, yogurt, almond milk, honey and vanilla extract mixing until completely smooth.
2. Add the oats, Chia seeds, and cinnamon and continue mixing until well blended.
3. Place the mixture in two containers and allow to sit for no less than 2 hours but overnight is best.
4. Serve this oatmeal cold*.

You can multiply this recipe in order to make more servings. This recipe will make 2 servings. The overnight oats will stay good in the fridge for up to 4 days. If you want the oats to be thinner, add a bit of almond milk just before serving.

Nutrition:
Serves: 1
- 370 calories per serving
- 16 grams of sugar
- 116 grams of sodium
- 13 grams of fat
- 53 grams of carbohydrates
- 9 grams of fiber
- 14 grams of protein

Kale and Sweet Potato Hash

Ingredients:

- 2 tablespoons of Extra Virgin Olive Oil
- 1 tablespoon of garlic, minced
- 1 sweet potato, peeled and diced
- 1 red bell pepper diced
- ½ of a yellow onion, diced
- 4 precooked chicken sausages, sliced
- 4 cups of kale stems removed
- 2 tablespoons of balsamic vinegar
- Salt and pepper

Method:

1. Begin by adding 1 tablespoon of the Extra Virgin Olive Oil to skillet over medium to high heat.
2. Add in the onion, sweet potato, red pepper, and chicken sausage.
3. Cook for about 7 minutes then add the kale as well as the rest of the oil.
4. Cook until the kale wilts.
5. Season with the balsamic vinegar and the salt and pepper.
6. Store and refrigerate in an airtight container.

Nutrition:

Serves: 4

- 251 calories per serving
- 8 grams of sugar
- 12 grams of fat
- 5 grams of fiber
- 16 grams of protein

Breakfast Burritos

Ingredients:

- 8 eggs
- A splash of milk
- 1 tablespoon of Extra Virgin Olive Oil
- 1 tablespoon of garlic minced
- 1 red bell pepper, minced
- ½ of a red onion, minced
- 4 pieces of bacon, precooked
- 4 flat tortilla shells
- Salt and pepper

Method:

1. Begin by placing the Extra Virgin Olive Oil in a saucepan along with the garlic over medium to high heat.
2. While the oil heats up, crack the eggs into a large bowl and add in just a splash of milk. Whisk. Set the eggs to the side.
3. Next, add the minced onion and pepper to the saucepan and allow to sauté for about 3 minutes.
4. Pour the egg and cook for another 3 to 5 minutes stirring constantly.
5. Place one slice of bacon on each tortilla shell and top with ¼ of the eggs.
6. You can also sprinkle cheese on this if desired.
7. Wrap the burrito and either freeze or eat them.

Nutrition:

Serves: 4

- 352 calories per serving
- 4 grams of sugar
- 20 grams of fat
- 22 grams of carbohydrates
- 9 grams of fiber
- 25 grams of protein

Best Peanut Butter Granola Bars

Ingredients:

- 1 cup of oat flour
- 1 cup of rolled oats
- ¼ of a cup of sea salt
- 2 tablespoons of ground flaxseed
- ½ of a cup of creamy peanut butter
- 1/3 of a cup of maple syrup
- 2 tablespoons of water
- ½ of a cup of chocolate chips if desired

Method:

1. Begin by preheating your oven to 350 degrees.
2. While the oven is preheating, spray an 8x8 baking pan with nonstick cooking spray.
3. Mix the oat flour, sea salt, oats, and ground flaxseed in a large bowl.
4. Add in the peanut butter and the maple syrup. Mix well. You can add the water if needed to reach the desired consistency.
5. If you are using the chocolate chips, add them in.
6. Wet your hands and spread the batter out in the baking pan that you have prepared.
7. Bake for 20 minutes and then let cool for another 20 minutes.
8. Cut this into 12 bars. These granola bars can be stored in an airtight container for 4 days or you can freeze them.

Nutrition:

Serves: 12

- 125 calories per serving
- 22 grams of carbohydrates
- 4 grams of fiber
- 8 grams of fat
- 14 grams of sugar

Gluten-Free, Vegan Waffles

Ingredients:
- 1 ¼ cups of unsweetened almond milk
- 1 teaspoon of Apple Cider Vinegar
- ¼ of a cup of coconut oil, melted
- ¼ of a cup of agave nectar
- ½ of a cup of gluten-free rolled oats
- 1 ¾ cups of gluten-free flour
- 1 ½ teaspoons of baking powder
- A pinch of salt
-

Add-ins:
- 1 teaspoon of vanilla extract
- ½ of a teaspoon of ground cinnamon
- 1 tablespoon of ground flaxseed
- ¼ of a cup of vegan chocolate chips
- ¼ of cup of fruit

Method:
1. Begin by mixing the Apple Cider Vinegar and the almond milk in a bowl.
2. Wait for it to curdle and then mix in the agave nectar, coconut oil, and maple syrup. Set to the side.
3. In a large bowl, you will mix the rolled oats, flour, baking powder, salt and any other DRY ingredients from the add-ins that you want to use.
4. Pour the wet ingredients into the dry and mix well.
5. You can add the vanilla extract and fruit at this point if desired.
6. Preheat your waffle iron for about 5 minutes.
7. Once the waffle iron has heated up, spray it with nonstick cooking spray and pour ½ of a cup of the batter on the waffle iron.
8. Cook according to the manufacturer's directions.
9. Serve immediately or place in a freezer bag and freeze.
10. These will stay good in the freezer for up to 2 months.

Nutrition:
- Serving size 1 waffle
- 301 calories per serving
- 9.7 grams of fat
- 1.4 grams of saturated fat
- 53 grams of carbohydrates
- 10 grams of sugar
- 44 milligrams of sodium
- 5.7 grams of fiber
- 5 grams of protein

Quinoa and Pesto Breakfast Bowl

Ingredients:

- 2 eggs
- 2 cups of quinoa, cooked
- ½ of an avocado
- ¼ of a cup of pesto
- 2 tablespoons of hemp seeds
- 1 tablespoon of Chia seeds
- 2 cups of basil leaves, fresh
- 1 cup of kale, fresh
- ¼ of a cup of nutritional yeast
- ¼ of a cup of pine nuts
- 1 clove of garlic
- 4 tablespoons of Extra Virgin Olive Oil
- 1 teaspoon of lemon juice
- Salt and pepper

Method:

1. Begin by boiling your eggs.
2. While the eggs boil, you will make your pesto using your food processor.
3. After the eggs have boiled, you will want to run cold water over them and then allow them to sit in the cold water for about 5 minutes.
4. While the eggs are cooling, place 1 cup of cooked quinoa in a bowl as well as ½ of the avocado, sliced thinly and half of the pesto.
5. After your eggs have cooled, you will peel them and slice them.
6. Place one egg in each bowl and sprinkle one-half of the Chia seeds as well as the hemp seeds over them.
7. Season with salt and pepper.
8. Store and refrigerate in an airtight container.

Nutrition:

- 246 calories per serving
- 9 grams of fat
- 13 grams of fiber
- 6 grams of sugar
- 21 grams of protein
- 26 grams of carbohydrates

Ham, Cauliflower Rice, and Kale Egg Muffins

Ingredients:
- 1 cup of cauliflower that has been cut into small bite sized bits
- 3 eggs
- 1 cup of kale torn into small pieces
- ¾ of a cup of ham diced small
- Salt and pepper

Method:
1. Begin by preheating your oven to 400 degrees.
2. While the oven preheats, spray your muffin tin with nonstick cooking spray and set to the side.
3. Place the cauliflower into your food processor and process until the cauliflower looks like rice.
4. Place the eggs in a large bowl and whisk.
5. Add in the cauliflower rice, ham, kale, salt, and pepper.
6. Blend well.
7. Divide the egg mixture into six in your muffin pan (you may find it easier to divide all of the ingredients except the eggs into the pan and then pour the eggs on top).
8. Bake for 20 minutes.
9. Let cool, eat fresh or store in an airtight container for later.

Nutrition:
- Serving size 1 muffin
- 204 calories per serving
- 9 grams of protein per serving
- 2 grams of fiber per serving

Peanut Butter and Chocolate Oatmeal Cups

Ingredients:

- 2 tablespoons of Chia seeds
- 6 tablespoons of water
- 3 bananas, mashed
- 1 cup of almond milk, unsweetened
- ¼ of a cup of creamy peanut butter
- ¼ of a cup of maple syrup or agave nectar
- 1 scoop of protein powder, plant based
- 3 cups of old fashioned oats
- 2 tablespoons of cocoa powder
- 1 tablespoon of baking powder
- ½ of a teaspoon of vanilla extract
- A pinch of salt

Method:

1. Begin by preheating your oven to 350 degrees
2. While the oven is preheating you will spray your muffin tin with nonstick cooking spray and set to the side.
3. Mix the Chia seeds and the water together in a small bowl and set to the side.
4. Place your bananas in a bowl and mash them, then add in the peanut butter, almond milk, agave nectar, and vanilla extract. Mix well.
5. Add in the Chia seeds that should have absorbed the water at this point as well as the oats, cocoa powder, protein powder, salt, and baking powder. Mix well.
6. Fill your muffin tins with the mixture and then bake for 25 minutes.
7. Allow it to cool and place in the fridge in an airtight container.

Nutrition:

- Serving size 1 muffin
- 115 calories per serving
- 5 grams of fat
- 21 carbohydrates
- 6 grams of sugar
- 4 grams of fiber
- 6 grams of protein

Breakfast Taco- Vegan Style

Ingredients:
For the tacos-
- 8 ounces of tofu, firm
- 1 cup of black beans, cooked
- ¼ of a red onion, minced
- 1 cup of chopped cilantro
- 1 avocado, sliced
- ½ of a cup of salsa
- 1 sliced lime
- ¼ of a cup of pomegranate arils
- 2 corn tortillas per person

For the Seasoning-
- ¾ of a teaspoon of garlic powder
- ½ of a teaspoon of chili powder
- 1 teaspoon of cumin
- 1/8 of a teaspoon of sea salt
- 1 tablespoon of salsa
- 1 tablespoon of water

Method:
1. Begin by wrapping your tofu in a towel that is absorbent and clean.
2. Place a heavy object on top of the wrapped tofu.
3. Heat your black beans in a saucepan on the stove.
4. Add the seasoning ingredients as well as the salsa to a bowl as well as enough water to make the mixture pourable. Set this to the side.
5. Place a large skillet on the stove over medium to high heat.
6. Take the tofu out of the towel and crumble with a fork.
7. Once the skillet is hot you will add 2 tablespoons of oil and the tofu to it.
8. Cook for about 5 minutes or until the tofu browns.
9. Add in the seasoning mixture. Stir well to coat the tofu.
10. Allow this to cook for about 10 more minutes, stirring occasionally. Set this to the side.
11. Warm your tortillas and then top them with the tofu scramble, the onion, avocado, black beans, cilantro, pomegranate arils, and the lime juice.
12. Store and refrigerate in an airtight container. This will make 4 servings.

Nutrition:
- Serving size 1 taco
- 259 calories 259
- 11 grams of fat
- 32 grams of carbohydrates
- 8 grams of sugar
- 9 grams of fiber
- 11 grams of protein

Eggs Benedict Casserole

Ingredients:
- 1 cup of egg whites or an egg substitute
- 2 ½ cups almond, soy, or cashew milk
- 1 pack of Hollandaise sauce mix
- ¾ of a teaspoon of salt
- ¼ of a teaspoon of black pepper
- 12 ounces of ham, chopped
- 12 ounces of frozen spinach that has been defrosted and then squeezed dry
- ½ of a cup of green onions, chopped
- 4 English Muffins, cut in half

Method:
1. Begin by preheating your oven to 350 degrees.
2. While the oven is preheating, spray your 13x9 inch baking dish with your favorite nonstick cooking spray. Set to the side.
3. Place the egg whites, milk, hollandaise sauce mix, salt, and pepper in a bowl.
4. Whisk together.
5. Add the spinach, ham, and green onions and then stir to ensure it is completely combined.
6. Pour the mixture into your baking dish.
7. Place the English muffins that you have cut in half on top of the mixture.
8. Place in the oven and bake for 45 minutes.
9. Rotate the dish after 23 minutes.
10. Once the timer is up, take the dish out and let it cool for 10 minutes.
11. Store and refrigerate in an airtight container.

Nutrition:
- For serving size 1/8th of the dish
- 233 calories 233
- 10 gram of fat
- 20 grams of carbohydrates
- 6 grams of fiber
- 1 gram of sugar
- 19 grams of protein

Apricot Energy Bars

Ingredients:
- 1 cup of chopped walnuts
- ½ of a cup of dried apricots
- ¼ of a cup of goji berries
- 1 tablespoon of fresh lemon juice
- 4 dates that have had the pits removed, and have soaked in water for 10 minutes
- The zest of 1 lemon
- 1 tablespoon of Chia seeds
- 1 tablespoon of hemp seeds

Method:
1. After the dates have soaked for 10 minutes, you will drain the water off of them.
2. Place all of the ingredients into your food processor and process them.
3. You want them to be almost smooth, but not completely smooth.
4. Pour the mixture into a baking dish and place in the freezer for 15 minutes.
5. Cut into bars and then place them in an airtight container in the fridge.

Nutrition:
- 136 calories per bar
- 2 grams of protein
- 4 grams of fiber

Egg, Polenta, and Refried Beans Skillet

Ingredients:

- Cooking spray
- 18 ounces of polenta
- ¼ of a cup of warm water
- 2 garlic cloves, minced
- ¼ of a teaspoon of salt
- Pepper to taste
- 15 ounces of refried beans
- ¾ of a cup of shredded cheddar
- 1 cup of chunky salsa
- 6 eggs
- Cilantro, avocado, or hot sauce to use as a garnish

Method:

1. Begin by preheating your oven to 375 degrees.
2. Spray your 9-inch cast iron skillet with your favorite nonstick cooking spray.
3. If you do not have a cast iron skillet, you can use a baking dish that is 9x9 as well.
4. Place the polenta in a large bowl and break it up.
5. Next, add in the salt, pepper, garlic, and water.
6. Use your hands to mix until everything is combined.
7. Place the polenta in the skillet or baking dish and pat it down.
8. Carefully spread the refried beans over the polenta, then spread the salsa on top of the refried beans.
9. Sprinkle the cheese over the salsa and crack the eggs on top of the cheese.
10. Place in the oven and bake for 35 minutes.
11. Garnish with cilantro, avocado, and hot sauce.
12. Store and refrigerate in an airtight container.

Nutrition:

Serves: 6

- 249 calories
- 7 grams of fat
- 31 grams of carbohydrates
- 4 grams of sugar
- 5 grams of fiber
- 15 grams of protein

Indian Baked Potato and Egg

Ingredients:

- 4 cups of golden yellow potatoes or sweet potatoes sliced
- ¼ of a cup of Extra Virgin Olive Oil
- ½ of a teaspoon of smoked paprika
- ½ of a teaspoon of garlic, minced
- ½ of a teaspoon of curry powder with turmeric
- ¼ of a teaspoon of salt
- ¼ of a teaspoon of pepper
- Foil
- 4 eggs
- Sriracha or red peppers- optional

Method:

1. Begin by preheating your oven to 400 degrees.
2. Slice the potatoes.
3. Place the olive oil and the seasonings in a bowl followed by the sliced potatoes.
4. Toss the potatoes to ensure they are coated evenly.
5. Place 1 cup of the coated potatoes on a piece of foil that is 8x8.
6. Fold and bake for 30 minutes.
7. Remove the foil, open, and crack the egg over the potatoes.
8. Close and place back into the oven for 10 more minutes.
9. Garnish with red peppers and Sriracha if desired.
10. Store and refrigerate in an airtight container.

Nutrition:

- 303 calories per pack
- 18 grams of fat
- 26 grams of carbohydrates
- 3 grams of fiber
- 10 grams of protein
- 2 grams of sugar

Blueberry Lemon Yogurt Breakfast Cake

Ingredients:

- 1 ½ cups of all-purpose flour
- 2 teaspoons of baking powder
- ½ of a teaspoon of salt
- 1 teaspoon of ground flaxseed
- 1 tablespoon of cornstarch
- ¾ of a cup of sugar
- 3 teaspoons of lemon zest
- 1/3 of a cup of vegetable oil
- 5.3 ounces of dairy free yogurt alternative (or yogurt)
- 1 tablespoon of ACV
- 1 cup of blueberries
- 6 tablespoons of fresh lemon juice
- 2 cups of powdered sugar

Method:

1. Begin by preheating your oven to 350 degrees and lining your loaf pan or spraying it with nonstick spray.
2. While the oven is preheating, place the baking powder, flour, flaxseed, cornstarch, and salt in a bowl and mix well. Set to the side.
3. Mix the sugar and the lemon zest in a separate bowl. Make sure this is mixed well.
4. In a third bowl, mix the yogurt, oil, and ACV. If you are using frozen blueberries you will want to sprinkle 1 tablespoon of the flour mixture over the top of them. If you are using fresh blueberries you do not need to do this.
5. Add the sugar mixture to the flour mixture. Stir.
6. Carefully fold the blueberries into the sugar and flour mixture, creating a batter.
7. Pour the batter into your loaf pan and bake for 50 minutes.
8. In the meantime, you will mix ½ of a cup of the powdered sugar with the lemon juice and stir well.
9. After the cake has cooked, allow it to cook for about 10 minutes.
10. Pour all of the lemon sauce except for 2 tablespoons over the cake.
11. Set the cake to the side.
12. Add the rest of the powdered sugar to the remaining lemon sauce and stir to create a glaze.
13. Drizzle the glaze over the cake when you serve it.
14. Store and refrigerate in an airtight container.

Nutrition:

- 387 calories per serving
- 10 grams of fat
- 73 grams of carbohydrates
- 1 gram of fiber
- 3 grams of protein
- 51 grams of sugar

Sea Salt and Dark Chocolate, Almond Banana Oatmeal Bake

Ingredients:
- 1 ¾ cups of rolled oats
- ½ of a cup of salted almonds, chopped roughly
- 1 teaspoon of baking powder
- 1 teaspoon of cinnamon
- 1 large banana, mashed
- 1 ¾ of a cup of almond milk, unsweetened
- 1 egg
- 1 ½ tablespoons of melted coconut oil
- 2 teaspoons of vanilla extract
- ¼ of a teaspoon of almond extract
- 1 ½ ounces of dark chocolate
- Sea salt
- Extra almonds and banana slices to top the oatmeal with

Method:
1. Begin by preheating your oven to 350 degrees and spray a 9x9 baking dish with nonstick cooking spray.
2. Place the oats, baking powder, almonds, and cinnamon in a large bowl and mix well.
3. Then mix the banana, vanilla extract, almond milk, almond extract, coconut oil, and egg in a separate bowl.
4. Pour the banana mixture into the dry ingredients and mix well.
5. Pour the batter into your baking dish and then sprinkle the chocolate on the top.
6. Bake this for 37 minutes.
7. Remove from oven and top with sea salt, banana slices, and chopped almonds.
8. Store and refrigerate in an airtight container. Serves six.
9. When you are reheating, you will want to add an extra tablespoon of milk to ensure that oatmeal is not too dry.

Nutrition:
- 267 calories per serving
- 15.2 grams of fat
- 27 grams of carbohydrates
- 6 grams of sugar
- 5 grams of fiber
- 7 grams of protein

Breakfast Cookie

Ingredients:
- 1 cup of mashed bananas (about 2 bananas)
- ½ of a cup of pumpkin puree
- 1/3 of a cup of coconut flour
- 4 soft dates
- 2 teaspoons of ground cinnamon
- ¼ of a teaspoon of ground ginger
- 1 teaspoon of baking soda
- 1 teaspoons of ACV
- ½ of a cup of unsweetened shredded coconut
- ½ of a cup of raisins

Method:
1. Begin by preheating your oven to 350 degrees.
2. Line your baking sheet with parchment paper.
3. Place the mashed bananas, dates, and pumpkin puree in the food processor and process until smooth.
4. Add in the cinnamon, baking soda, ginger, vinegar, and coconut flour.
5. Continue to process until everything is mixed well.
6. Fold the coconut and the raisins into the mixture and using a tablespoon scoop it onto the baking sheet.
7. You will want to flatten the cookies a bit because they are not going to spread while baking.
8. Bake the cookies for 25 minutes.
9. Allow them to cook in the pan for 15 minutes before removing them so that they do not fall apart because they are very soft.
10. These can be stored in an airtight container in the refrigerator for up to one week.

Nutrition:
- Serving size 1 cookie
- 100 calories

Avocado and Egg Bowl

Ingredients:
- 2 hard-boiled eggs that have been cut into chunks
- ½ of an avocado, cut into chunks
- 1 tablespoon of finely chopped red onion
- 1 tablespoon of finely chopped red pepper
- Salt and pepper to taste

Method:
1. Place the avocado, eggs, red pepper, and onion in a bowl.
2. Season with salt and pepper.
3. Store and refrigerate in an airtight container.

Nutrition:
- 295 calories 295
- 21 grams of fat
- 12 grams of protein
- 8 grams of fiber
- 4 grams of sugar
- 15 grams of protein

Parfait

Ingredients:

- 2 cups of granola
- 2 cups of your favorite Greek yogurt
- 4 cups of your favorite fresh berries

Method:

1. Begin by placing ½ of a cup of granola in the bottom of your container followed by ½ of a cup of yogurt and 1 cup of berries.
2. Repeat.

Blueberry Chia Seed Pudding

Ingredients:

- ¾ of a cup of blueberries
- ¼ of a cup of chia seeds
- ½ of a cup of Vanilla flavored Greek yogurt
- 1 cup of unsweetened almond milk
- 1 teaspoon of vanilla extract
- 2 tablespoons of agave nectar
- 1 teaspoon of fresh lemon juice

Method:

1. Begin by smashing the blueberries with a fork and then mix in the rest of the ingredients.
2. Place in the fridge for 6 hours, stirring every couple of hours.
3. If you want a fluffy pudding, after the pudding has sat in the fridge for 6 hours, pour it into the blender and blend well.
4. Top with lemon zest and blueberries.
5. Store and refrigerate in an airtight container.

Banana Pancakes

Ingredients:

- 1 ½ cups of whole wheat flour
- 1 teaspoon of baking powder
- ½ of a teaspoon of ground cinnamon
- 1/8 of a teaspoon of salt
- 2 bananas that have been mashed
- 2 eggs
- 1 teaspoon of vanilla extract
- 1 cup of almond milk
- 3 tablespoons of melted coconut oil

Method:

1. Begin by spraying your skillet with nonstick cooking spray and place over medium heat.
2. Mix the flour, baking powder, cinnamon, and salt in a large bowl.
3. In a separate bowl, mix the mashed bananas, eggs, milk, and vanilla extract.
4. Whisk together until very smooth.
5. Slowly mix the dry ingredients into the wet ingredients mixing as you add them in.
6. Pour the coconut oil into the mixture and stir until smooth.
7. Pour ¼ of a cup of the batter into your skillet and cook for 3 minutes on each side.
8. Store and refrigerate in an airtight container.

Nutrition:

Serves: 12

- For serving size 1 pancake
- 122 calories 122
- 3 grams of sugar
- 5 grams of fat
- 3 grams of fiber
- 3 grams of protein

Lunches:

Chicken and Rainbow Veggies

Ingredients:
- 2 boneless, skinless chicken breasts, cut into pieces that are about ½ of an inch in size
- 1 cup of broccoli florets
- 1 chopped red onion
- 1 cup of plum tomatoes
- 1 chopped zucchini
- 2 garlic cloves, minced
- 1 tablespoon of Italian seasoning
- 1 teaspoon of salt
- ½ of a teaspoon of black pepper
- ½ of a teaspoon of red pepper flakes
- ½ of a teaspoon of paprika
- 2 tablespoons of Extra Virgin Olive Oil
- 4 cups of cooked brown rice
- 4 containers

Method:
1. Begin by preheating your oven to 450 degrees and lining your baking sheet with foil.
2. Set to the side.
3. Place the chicken and the vegetables on the baking sheet and drizzle the extra virgin olive oil over them.
4. Sprinkle the spices over the chicken and the vegetables and then bake for 20 minutes.
5. While the chicken is baking, place 1 of a cup of the precooked rice in each container.
6. After the chicken is done you will divide it as well as the vegetables evenly among the containers placing them on the rice.
7. Cover and place in the fridge or freezer.
8. This will stay good for 5 days in the fridge or 2 months in the freezer.

Nutrition:
- 240 calories 240
- 15 grams of fat
- 7 grams of carbohydrates
- 3 grams of sugar
- 20 grams of protein

Sweet Potato and Chicken Bowls

Ingredients:
- 2 pounds of boneless, skinless chicken breasts that are cut into bite sized pieces
- 1 tablespoon of honey
- 2 teaspoons of paprika
- 2 teaspoons of cumin
- 2 teaspoons of salt
- 2 teaspoons of pepper
- The juice from 2 lemons
- 4 cloves of garlic, minced
- A pinch of red pepper flakes
- 5 tablespoons of Extra Virgin Olive Oil
- 2 sweet potatoes cut into thin 'fries'
- 1 bunch of asparagus that has been trimmed
- 4 cups of quinoa, pre-cooked
- ½ of a cup of Kalamata olives pitted
- ½ of a cup of sun-dried tomatoes packed in oil, drained
- Shredded lettuce, avocado, goat cheese, sliced cucumbers, pine nuts, red onions, mint, lemons, or cilantro to garnish

For the Tahini Yogurt
- 1 cup of Greek yogurt, plain
- 2 tablespoons of tahini
- 2 cloves of garlic, minced
- The juice from ½ of a lemon
- 1 tablespoon of chopped mint

Method:
1. Begin by placing the chicken in a gallon sized storage bag.
2. Add in the 2 tablespoons of Extra Virgin Olive Oil, red pepper flakes, garlic, lemon juice, salt, cumin, pepper, paprika, and honey.
3. Seal and toss to coat the chicken. Leave sealed in the fridge for 12 hours.
4. Preheat your oven to 425 degrees, then place your sweet potato matchsticks on a baking sheet.
5. Drizzle with 2 teaspoons of Extra Virgin Olive oil.
6. Sprinkle with salt and pepper, then toss to coat evenly.
7. Place in the oven for 20 minutes.
8. After 20 minutes, flip the potatoes and cook for an additional 20 minutes.
9. On a separate baking sheet, you will toss the asparagus with 1 tablespoon of Extra Virgin Olive oil, pepper and salt, then bake for 15 minutes.
10. Place the chicken on a third baking sheet and bake for 20 minutes.
11. While everything is baking you will divide your quinoa between 6 containers.
12. After all of the food has cooked, divide the chicken and vegetables amongst the containers.
13. Keep in the fridge for up to 7 days.
14. Before serving, mix all of the ingredients for the Tahini yogurt and drizzle over the top of the bowl after it has been heated.

Pesto Chicken Pockets

Ingredients:
- 2 boneless, skinless chicken breasts
- 1 tablespoon of Extra Virgin Olive Oil
- Salt and pepper
- 6 cups of mixed vegetables that have been chopped
- Red onion
- Bell pepper
- Zucchini
- 1 tablespoon of Extra Virgin Olive oil
- 1/3 of a cup of pesto
- 4 pita pockets

Method:
1. Begin by preheating your oven to 425 degrees.
2. Toss the chicken with 1 tablespoon of EVOO, sprinkle with salt and pepper and place on a baking sheet.
3. Toss the vegetables with 1 tablespoon of EVOO, sprinkle with salt and pepper and place on a separate baking sheet.
4. Place both baking sheets in the oven and cook for 10 minutes.
5. Flip the chicken and the vegetables, cook both for 15 more minutes.
6. Let the chicken rest for 10 minutes and then slice it into strips.
7. Place the chicken and the vegetables into a bowl, add the pesto and mix well, ensuring everything is coated.
8. Divide the mixture into 4 separate containers, leaving the pita separate.
9. When ready to serve, cut the pita in half and open it spooning the mixture into the pita.

Nutrition:
For serving size: 1 pita pocket
- 449 calories 449
- 18 grams of fat
- 40 grams of carbohydrates
- 4 grams of fiber
- 3 grams of sugar
- 29 grams of protein

Chicken and Cauliflower Rice

Ingredients:
For the chicken
- 1 pound of boneless, skinless chicken breast
- 2 tablespoons of extra virgin olive oil
- Salt and pepper
- ¼ of a cup of lime juice
- 1/3 of a cup of chopped cilantro
- 2 tablespoons of garlic, minced
- 1/8 of a teaspoon of sea salt
- ½ of a teaspoon of honey

For the rice
- 2 tablespoons of Extra Virgin Olive Oil
- 3 cups of cauliflower rice
- 2 teaspoons of garlic powder
- 1 teaspoon of cumin
- 1/8 of a teaspoon of sea salt
- ½ of a cup of black beans
- ¼ of a cup of chopped red onion

Method:
For the chicken
1. Begin by heating the olive oil in a skillet over medium heat.
2. Once the oil has heated, you will add the chicken and cook for about 7 minutes, turn and cook for another 7 minutes.
3. Allow the chicken to cool for 20 minutes before you slice it.
4. After you slice the chicken set it to the side.
5. Add the rest of the ingredients for the chicken into a bowl and mix well.
6. Add the chicken, toss, and place in the refrigerator.

For the rice
1. Heat the olive oil in a skillet over medium heat.
2. After the oil has heated, add in the cauliflower rice as well as the spices, mix well and cook for about 5 minutes.
3. Add the black beans, cook for an additional 2 minutes and then add in the onion.
4. Mix well.
5. Place the cauliflower rice in 4 containers, top with the chicken.
6. You can also add in ¼ of a cup of tomatoes to each container as well as ¼ of a cup of avocado.
7. You can keep this in the fridge for up to 4 days.

Nutrition:
- 378 calories per serving
- 6 grams of sugar
- 21 grams of fat
- 16 grams of carbohydrates
- 7 grams of fiber
- 32 grams of protein

Fiesta Chicken Bowls

Ingredients:
- 1 tablespoon of EVOO
- 4 boneless, skinless chicken breasts
- 1 teaspoon of salt
- 1 tablespoon of chili powder
- 1 teaspoon of garlic powder
- 1 teaspoon of cumin
- ½ of a cup of corn
- 2 sliced red onions
- 1 red bell pepper, diced
- 1 green bell pepper, diced
- 1 yellow bell pepper, diced
- 2 cups of brown rice, cooked
- ¾ of a cup of salsa
- 1/3 of a cup of chopped cilantro
- ¼ of a cup of feta cheese

Method:
1. Begin by placing the EVOO in a skillet and heating over medium to high heat.
2. Place the chicken in the skillet and cook for 2 minutes, add salt if desired.
3. After 2 minutes, add the cumin, garlic powder, and chili powder.
4. Toss and continue to cook for 4 minutes.
5. Add in the corn, onion, and all peppers.
6. Cook for an additional 4 minutes.
7. Add the salsa and the cooked brown rice.
8. Cook for another 5 minutes.
9. Add in cilantro and remove from the heat.
10. Sprinkle feta cheese on top.
11. Store and refrigerate in an airtight container.

Nutrition:
Serves: 4
- 407 calories per serving
- 12 grams of fat
- 47 grams of carbohydrates
- 33 grams of protein

Chicken Burrito Bowls

Ingredients:

- 2 cups of kale, stems removed
- 1 cup of grape tomatoes
- 3 cups of shredded chicken
- ¾ of a cup of canned corn
- 1 ½ of a cup of canned black beans, drained and rinsed
- 1 cup of cooked brown rice
- 1 teaspoon of paprika
- ½ of a teaspoon of cumin
- ¼ of a teaspoon of cayenne
- ¼ of a teaspoon of black pepper

Method:

1. Mix the cumin, paprika, cayenne, and black pepper in the cooked rice then set to the side.
2. Dividing between 4 containers, place the kale on the bottom of each followed by the beans, corn, and then rice.
3. Top with chicken.
4. Store and refrigerate in an airtight container.

Nutrition:

- 301 calories per serving

Chicken and Veggie Bowl

Ingredients:

- 16 ounces of pre-cooked quinoa
- 16 ounces of pre-cooked brown rice
- 4 cups of chopped roasted asparagus
- 4 cups of roasted broccoli
- 4 cups of roasted cauliflower
- 4 cups of shredded chicken

Method:

1. You will need 8 separate containers.
2. Place ¼ of a cup of quinoa, as well as ¼ of a cup of brown rice into each container.
3. Follow this with ¼ of a cup of each vegetable and ¼ of a cup of shredded chicken.
4. You can also add salsa or hot sauce if desired.

Red Pepper and Quinoa Chili

Ingredients:

- 1 cup of quinoa
- 2 cups of water
- 12 ounces of roasted red peppers
- 1 red bell pepper, chopped
- ½ of a red onion, diced
- 1 Serrano pepper, diced
- 1 tablespoon of garlic, minced
- 28 ounces of crushed tomatoes
- 15 ounces of white northern beans, drained and rinsed
- 15 ounces of kidney beans, drained and rinsed
- 4 tablespoons of chili powder
- ½ of a teaspoon of sea salt
- 1 teaspoon of cumin
- 2 teaspoons of garlic powder
- 2 teaspoons of agave nectar

Method:

1. Cook the quinoa according to the directions on the package.
2. As the quinoa is cooking, you will place the 12 ounces of roasted red peppers as well as the liquid in your food processor and puree. Set this to the side.
3. When the quinoa begins boiling, you will add in the rest of the ingredients.
4. Stir, cover the mixture and allow it to boil for 15 minutes, reduce the heat to low and simmer for 15 more minutes.
5. Store and refrigerate in an airtight container.
6. Serve this with chopped green onions, plain Greek yogurt, and tortilla chips.

Nutrition:

Serves: 6

- 295 calories per serving
- 15 grams of sugar
- 2 grams of fat
- 56 grams of carbohydrates
- 12 grams of fiber
- 14 grams of protein

Cashew Chicken and Quinoa

Ingredients:
- 1 cup of uncooked quinoa, rinsed
- 1 cup of minced yellow onion
- 2 red bell peppers, chopped
- 16 ounces of boneless, skinless chicken breast chopped
- ½ of a cup of hoisin sauce
- 1 tablespoon of garlic, minced
- 2 tablespoons of soy sauce
- ½ of a tablespoon of minced ginger
- 1 cup of water
- 1 cup of roasted cashews
- Green onion to garnish

Method:
1. Begin by preheating your oven to 375 degrees.
2. Spray your baking dish with nonstick cooking spray.
3. Place the quinoa in the bottom of the baking dish, top with onion and then red pepper.
4. Place the chicken on top of the vegetables.
5. In a bowl, mix the garlic, hoisin sauce, soy sauce, 1 cup of water, and ginger.
6. Whisk well. Pour the sauce evenly over the chicken.
7. Bake for 45 minutes.
8. Top the chicken with the cashews and bake for 10 more minutes.
9. Store and refrigerate in an airtight container.
10. You can garnish this with the green onion.

Nutrition:
Serves: 4
- 457 calories per serving
- 15 grams of sugar
- 10 grams of fat
- 54 grams of carbohydrates
- 5 grams of fiber
- 37 grams of protein

No Mayo Tuna Salad

Ingredients:
- 1 avocado
- ¼ of a cup of Greek yogurt, plain
- ½ of a cup of minced garlic
- ½ of a teaspoon of onion powder
- ¼ of a teaspoon of sea salt
- ¼ of a teaspoon of black pepper
- 1 tablespoon of relish
- 8 ounces of tuna packed in water, or tuna pouch
- 1 stalk of celery, chopped
- ½ of a red onion, chopped
- The juice of ½ of a lemon

Method:
1. Begin by placing the Greek yogurt and the avocado in a bowl.
2. Mix them together using a fork and mashing the avocado.
3. Once the mixture is smooth, you will add in the salt, pepper, relish, onion powder, and the garlic.
4. Mix well.
5. Add the onion, celery, and tuna.
6. Mix until completely combined.
7. Add in the lemon juice and stir well.
8. You can serve this on crackers, with vegetables, or on a sandwich.
9. This can be stored in an airtight container in the refrigerator for up to 2 days.

Nutrition:
Serves: 4
- 117 calories per serving
- 4 grams of fat
- 4 grams of carbohydrates
- 2 grams of fiber
- and 18 grams of protein

Greek Chicken Salad in a Jar

Ingredients:
- 5 mason jars that are 1 quart in size
- 10 tablespoons of olive oil and vinegar dressing (Newman's Own works well)
- 1 quart of cherry tomatoes, cut in half
- 5 pickle sized cucumbers, sliced
- 1 cup of olives, pitted and chopped
- ¾ of a cup of feta cheese, crumbled
- 2 cups of shredded chicken breast
- 5 cups of romaine lettuce, chopped

Method:
1. Divide all of the ingredients between the 5 jars and layer them in starting with the dressing.
2. Next layer the tomatoes, followed by the cucumber slices, olives, feta, shredded chicken and top with the lettuce.
3. Place the lid on the jar and place in the fridge.
4. When you are ready to eat the salad, simply pour it into a bowl.
5. You can make these salads up to 6 days in advance.

Nutrition:
- 449 calories per serving
- 33 grams of fat
- 14 grams of carbohydrates
- 4 grams of fiber
- 24 grams of protein

Pasta Salad in a Jar

Ingredients:

- 5 mason jars
- 10 tablespoons of balsamic vinegar salad dressing
- 1 quart of grape tomatoes halved
- 10 ounces of mozzarella cheese, fresh
- 2 cups of cooked whole grain pasta
- 10 cups of baby spinach

Method:

1. Divide the ingredients between the five jars starting with the salad dressing followed by the tomatoes, then the mozzarella, whole grain pasta and top with the spinach.
2. Place the lid on the jar.
3. When you are ready to eat, shake the jar and pour it into a bowl.
4. You can make these 7 days in advance.

Nutrition:

- 382 calories per serving
- 22 grams of fat
- 30 grams of carbohydrates
- 6 grams of fiber
- 22 grams of protein

Dinners:

All of the recipes in this chapter can be made in advance and stored in the refrigerator. They can also be prepared as freezer meals.

Mushroom Bolognese

Ingredients:
- ½ of an ounce of porcini mushrooms
- 1 cup of boiling water
- 1 tablespoon of EVOO
- 2 ½ cups of onion, chopped
- ¾ of a teaspoon of salt
- ½ of a teaspoon of black pepper
- ½ of a pound of ground pork
- 8 cups of cremini mushrooms, chopped finely
- 1 tablespoon of garlic, minced
- 2 tablespoons of tomato paste
- ½ of a cup of white wine
- 14 ounces of whole peeled tomatoes and the juice
- ¼ of a cup of milk
- 10 ounces of whole-wheat spaghetti, uncooked
- 1 tablespoon of salt
- 1 ½ ounces of Parmigianino-Reggiano, grated
- ¼ of a cup of chopped parsley

Method:
1. Begin by mixing the boiling water and the porcini in a bowl.
2. Cover the mixture and set to the side for 20 minutes.
3. After the porcini is soft, you will drain it, reserving the liquid for later.
4. Chop the porcini.
5. Place the EVOO in the bottom of a Dutch oven and heat over medium to high heat.
6. Once the oil has heated, add in the onion, ¼ of a teaspoon of pepper, ½ of a teaspoon of salt, and the ground pork.
7. Cook until the pork has browned or for about 10 minutes.
8. Stir the pork while it is cooking to crumble it.
9. Add in the cremini mushrooms, ¼ of a teaspoon of salt, garlic, and the remaining black pepper.
10. Cook this for about 15 minutes.
11. The liquid should be almost completely gone, then add in the porcini.
12. Continue to cook for 1 minute.
13. Add the tomato paste and stir.
14. Cook for another 2 minutes.
15. Add in the porcini liquid that you reserved as well as the wine and allow to cook for 1 minutes.
16. Stir constantly scraping the brown bits from the bottom of the pan.
17. Add the tomatoes, stir and bring the mixture to a boil.
18. Reduce the heat to low and let simmer for about 30 minutes.
19. Stir occasionally and break up the tomatoes if desired.

20. After 30 minutes, add the milk. Stir. Cook for an additional 2 minutes.
21. Cook the spaghetti according to the directions on the box, adding in a tablespoon of salt to the water as it cooks.
22. After you drain the pasta, toss it into the Dutch oven and top with the cheese.
23. Store and refrigerate in an airtight container.

Nutrition:

Serves: 6

- 344 calories per serving
- 9 grams of fat
- 22 grams of protein
- 50 grams of carbohydrates
- 10 grams of fiber

Bourbon Peach Butter Grilled Chicken

Ingredients:
- 1 ½ pounds of peaches, peeled and chopped coarsely
- ¼ of a cup of lemon juice
- 3 tablespoons of water
- ½ of a cup of bourbon
- 1/3 of a cup of brown sugar, packed
- ¾ of a teaspoon of salt
- ½ of a teaspoon of black pepper
- 36 ounces of boneless, skinless chicken breasts
- Nonstick cooking spray

Method:
1. Begin by preheating your oven to 250 degrees.
2. Mix the peaches, lemon juice, and water in a large saucepan.
3. Bring the mixture to a boil and cover.
4. Reduce the heat to low and allow to cook for 30 minutes.
5. Place the peach mixture in your food processor as well as the brown sugar, bourbon, and ¼ of a teaspoon of the salt.
6. Process until it is smooth.
7. Pour the mixture into a 13x9 baking dish.
8. Bake for 2 hours.
9. Preheat your grill to medium to high heat.
10. Sprinkle the salt and pepper that is remaining over your chicken.
11. Coat your grill with nonstick cooking spray and place the chicken on it.
12. Grill on each side for about 6 minutes, then top it with the sauce.
13. Store and refrigerate in an airtight container.

Nutrition:
Serves: 6
- 304 calories per serving
- 2.5 grams of fat
- 41 grams of protein
- 24 grams of carbohydrates
- 2 grams of fiber

Carrots and Chickpea Couscous

Ingredients:

- ¼ of a cup of vegetable broth
- 1 tablespoon of lemon zest
- 3 tablespoons of lemon juice
- 1 tablespoon of tomato paste
- 31 ounces of garbanzo beans, drained and rinsed
- 3 tablespoons of canola oil
- 1 cup of red bell pepper, chopped
- 1 cup of carrots, julienne
- 1 jalapeno pepper, chopped finely
- 1 teaspoon of cumin seeds
- ¼ of a teaspoon of salt
- ¼ of a teaspoon of pepper
- ¼ of a teaspoon of allspice
- 1/8 of a teaspoon of red pepper, ground
- 6 cloves of garlic, minced
- 4 cups of couscous, cooked
- ½ of a cup of cilantro
- Lemon cut into wedges

Method:

1. Begin by placing the first 4 ingredients in a bowl and whisking together.
2. Place the chickpeas on a paper towel to dry.
3. Place 2 tablespoons of oil in a skillet. Heat over high heat and make sure that the bottom of the pan is coated in oil.
4. Place the chickpeas in the skillet and cook for about 3 minutes.
5. Remove the chickpeas and set to the side.
6. Wipe the pan out using a paper towel.
7. Add the rest of the oil, ensuring that the bottom of the pan is completely coated.
8. Heat over high heat and then add in the jalapeno, carrots and bell pepper.
9. Cook for about 2 minutes, stirring occasionally.
10. Add the cumin seeds, ¼ of a teaspoon of salt, ¼ of a teaspoon of pepper, ¼ of a teaspoon of allspice, ground red pepper, and six cloves of garlic to the pan and cook for an additional 30 seconds.
11. Add the broth mixture that you sat to the side previously as well as the chickpeas.
12. Bring this to a boil and then remove it from the heat.
13. Mix in the couscous, cilantro and lemon wedges.
14. Store and refrigerate in an airtight container.

Nutrition:

Serves: 4

- 420 calories per serving
- 13 grams of fat
- 65 grams of carbohydrates
- 9 grams of fiber
- 13 grams of protein

Pulled Pork Sandwiches

Ingredients:
- 3 pounds of boneless pork roast
- Salt
- 2/3 of a cup of ACV
- 1 ½ cups of your favorite BBQ sauce as well as extra for serving
- 6 buns
- 2 cups of coleslaw

Method:
1. Begin by trimming the fat from the roast and then sprinkle it with the salt.
2. Place the roast in your crockpot and pour the ACV over it.
3. Place the lid on the crockpot and cook for about 10 hours.
4. Remove the roast and use two forks to shred the meat.
5. Discard the liquid in the crockpot. Place the meat back in the crockpot and add in the barbecue sauce.
6. Place the lid on the crockpot and allow to cook for another 30 minutes.
7. When you are ready to serve the sandwiches, you will begin by spooning the coleslaw onto the bun, add the pork as well as any extra barbecue sauce.
8. Add the top bun.
9. Store and refrigerate in an airtight container.

Nutrition:
Serves: 6
- 578 calories per serving
- 21 grams of fat
- 51 grams of protein
- 42 grams of carbohydrates
- 3 grams of fiber

Pot Roast and Turnip Greens

Ingredients:

- ¾ of a cup of all-purpose flour
- 3 pounds of boneless chuck roast, fat trimmed off
- 1 teaspoon of salt
- ½ of a teaspoon of pepper
- 1 tablespoon of EVOO
- 1 pound of turnip greens, chopped coarsely
- 3 parsnips, cut diagonally
- 3 cups of Yukon potatoes, peeled and cubed
- 2 cups of onions, peeled and chopped
- 2 tablespoons of tomato paste
- 1 cup of red wine
- 14 ounces of beef broth
- 1 tablespoon of black peppercorns
- 4 sprigs of thyme
- 3 cloves of garlic, crushed
- 2 bay leaves
- 1 bunch of parsley

Method:

1. Begin by placing the flour in a dish.
2. Then sprinkle the roast with salt and pepper.
3. Dredge the beef in the flour.
4. Place a large skillet on the stove over medium to high heat.
5. Add in the oil, ensuring that the bottom of the pan is coated.
6. Place the beef in the pan and sauté on each side for 10 minutes.
7. Place the turnip greens in your crockpot, followed by the potatoes, parsnips, and the onions.
8. Place the beef on top of the vegetables.
9. Add the tomato paste into the skillet that you browned the beef in.
10. Stirring this constantly you will cook it for about 30 seconds.
11. Add in the wine as well as the broth. Bring this to a boil, stirring it to ensure that you scrape all of the brown bits off of the bottom of the pan.
12. Cook for 1 minute after it begins to boil and then pour it over the beef.
13. Place the peppercorns, thyme, garlic, bay leaves, and the parsley in the center of a cheese cloth and create a seasoning bag by bringing the corners together and tying.
14. Place the bag in the slow cooker.
15. Place the lid on the slow cooker and cook on low heat for 8 hours.
16. After 8 hours, take out the spice bag and discard.
17. Remove the roast, slice it and add the meat with the vegetables to the side.
18. Store and refrigerate in an airtight container.

Nutrition:

Serves: 12

- 424 calories per serving
- 22 grams of fat
- 33 grams of protein
- 24 grams of carbohydrates
- 3 grams of fiber

Beef Daube

Ingredients:

- 2 pounds of boneless chuck roast, fat trimmed and then cut into bite sized chunks
- 1 tablespoon of EVOO
- 6 cloves of garlic, minced
- ½ of a cup of boiling water
- ½ of an ounce of porcini mushrooms
- ¾ of a teaspoon of salt
- Nonstick cooking spray
- ½ of a cup of red wine
- ¼ of a cup of beef broth
- 1/3 of a cup of Nicoise olives, pitted
- ½ of a teaspoon of black pepper
- 2 carrots, peeled and sliced thinly
- 1 onion, chopped
- 1 stalk of celery, sliced thinly
- 15 ounces of whole tomatoes, drained and then crushed
- 1 teaspoon of black peppercorns
- 3 parsley sprigs
- 3 thyme sprigs
- 1 bay leaf
- 1 strip of orange rind that is 1-inch wide
- 1 tablespoon of water
- 1 teaspoon of cornstarch
- 1 ½ tablespoons of chopped parsley
- 1 ½ tablespoons of chopped thyme

Method:

1. Begin by placing the first 3 ingredients in the list in a gallon sized storage bag.
2. Seal the bag and let the meat marinate for 30 minutes at room temperature.
3. Turn the bag every 10 minutes.
4. Next, place the water and the mushrooms in a bowl, cover and allow to sit for 30 minutes.
5. Drain the mushrooms and save ¼ of a cup of the water.
6. Chop the mushrooms.
7. Place a skillet over medium to high heat and coat with nonstick cooking spray.
8. Sprinkle the beef with ¼ of a teaspoon of salt and then add half of the beef to the skillet.
9. Cook for 5 minutes, browning it on all sides.
10. Once the beef is browned, place it in the crockpot.
11. Repeat this with the other half of the beef.
12. After all of the beef has cooked, add the broth and the wine to the skillet, bringing it to a boil.

13. Make sure that you stir it and scrape all of the brown bits off of the bottom of the pan.
14. After the liquid begins to boil, add in the ¼ of a cup of reserved mushroom water, mushrooms, the rest of the salt, the olives, black pepper, carrots, onions, celery, and tomatoes.
15. Place the parsley sprigs, the bay leaf, thyme, peppercorns, and the orange rind in the center of a cheesecloth.
16. Bring the edges up and tie them with twine to create a spice bag.
17. Pour the wine mixture into the crockpot and place the spice bag in the liquid.
18. Place the lid on the crockpot and cook on low heat for 6 hours.
19. After 6 hours, remove the spice bag.
20. Mix the cornstarch and the tablespoon of water in a bowl and mix until it is completely smooth.
21. Add the slurry to the crockpot and mix well.
22. Allow to cook for another 20 minutes.
23. Top with the chopped thyme and parsley.
24. Store and refrigerate in an airtight container.

Nutrition:
Serves: 8

- 360 calories per serving
- 22 grams of fat
- 31 grams of protein
- 8 grams of carbohydrates
- 3 grams of fat

Pasta with Meat Sauce

Ingredients:

- 1 tablespoon of EVOO
- 2 cups of onions, chopped
- 1 cup of carrots, chopped
- 6 cloves of garlic, minced
- 8 ounces of hot Italian sausage that has had the casing removed
- 1 pound of sirloin, ground
- ½ of a cup of pitted Kalamata olives, sliced
- ¼ of cup of tomato paste
- 1 ½ teaspoons of sugar
- 1 teaspoon of salt
- ½ of a teaspoon of crushed red pepper
- 28 ounces of crushed tomatoes, with the liquid
- 1 cup of tomato sauce
- 1 tablespoon of oregano, chopped
- 18 ounces of MAF Aldine pasta, uncooked
- ½ of a cup of basil, torn into pieces
- 3 ounces of Parmigiano-Reggiano, shaved

Method:

1. Begin by placing a large skillet on the stove over medium to high heat.
2. Add the oil, ensuring that it coats the bottom of the pan.
3. Allow the oil to heat and then add in the carrots and the onions.
4. Cook for 4 minutes. Stir occasionally.
5. Add in the garlic and continue to cook for 1 minute.
6. Pour the carrot mixture into your crockpot.
7. Place the sausage and the beef into your skillet and cook for about 6 minutes. Make sure that you stir it constantly so that it crumbles.
8. Using a slotted spoon, remove the beef mixture from the skillet and place it on paper towels, to drain.
9. After it drains, add it to the crockpot.
10. Stir in the olives, tomato paste, sugar, salt, red pepper, crushed tomatoes, and tomato sauce.
11. Place the lid on the crockpot and cook on low heat for 8 hours.
12. After 8 hours, stir the oregano in.
13. Then cook the pasta following the directions on the package but omit the fat and the salt.
14. Place the pasta in a bowl, top with meat sauce, cheese, and basil.
15. Store and refrigerate in an airtight container.

Nutrition:

Serves: 8

- 503 calories per serving
- 17 grams of fat
- 27 grams of protein
- 60 grams of carbohydrates
- 6 grams of fiber

Pork Posole

Ingredients:

1 teaspoon of EVOO
12 ounces of pork shoulder roast, fat trimmed and cut into bite sized pieces
1 cup of onion, chopped
4 cloves of garlic, minced
1 ½ teaspoons of cumin
½ of a teaspoon of red pepper flakes
½ of a cup of beer
2 cups of chicken stock
½ of a cup of salsa verde
28 ounces of hominy, drained and rinsed
¼ of a cup of cilantro
4 sliced radishes
1 lime, cut into 4 wedges

Method:

1. Begin by placing your Dutch oven over medium to high heat.
2. Add the oil into the bottom of the Dutch oven making sure that it covers the bottom.
3. Add in the chopped pork.
4. Cook for 5 minutes, stirring so that it browns on all sides.
5. Remove the pork from the Dutch oven and set to the side.
6. Reserve a tablespoon of the drippings that are in the pan.
7. Add the onion into the Dutch oven and cook for 4 minutes, then add in the garlic, cooking for an additional minute.
8. Place the pork back into the Dutch oven and then add in the pepper as well as the cumin.
9. Stir.
10. Add the beer to the Dutch oven and bring the mixture to a boil.
11. Cook for about 9 minutes or until the liquid has almost evaporated.
12. Pour the chicken stock and the salsa into the Dutch oven, then add in the hominy.
13. Bring the mixture to a boil.
14. Place the lid on the Dutch oven to reduce the heat to low and cook for 1 hour.
15. Place 1 1/3 cups of the mixture into each bowl.
16. Garnish with cilantro, radish, and a lime wedge.
17. Store and refrigerate in an airtight container.

Nutrition:

Serves: 4

- 231 calories per serving
- 6 grams of fat
- 14 grams of protein
- 30 grams of carbohydrates
- 6 grams of fiber

Root Vegetable Pot Pie

Ingredients:
- ½ of a cup of morels, dried
- 2 cups of vegetable broth
- 1 pound of portabella mushrooms
- 1 tablespoon of butter
- ½ of a cup of shallots, chopped
- ½ of a teaspoon of thyme
- ¼ of a teaspoon of sage
- 1 head of fennel
- 1 ½ pounds of red potatoes, scrubbed and cut into chunks
- 3 turnips, peeled and cut into chunks
- ½ of a cup of white wine
- 1 ½ tablespoons of cornstarch
- ¼ of a cup of heavy whipping cream
- 1 cup of spinach, chopped
- Salt and pepper to taste

Method:
1. Begin by placing the morels in a bowl that is microwave safe, top with the vegetable broth and cook in the microwave for 8 minutes.
2. Allow to stand for an additional 10 minutes.
3. While the morels are soaking, clean your portabella mushrooms, trim them and discard any discolored pieces.
4. Wash the mushrooms in water quickly. You do not want the mushrooms to soak because they will absorb the water.
5. Chop the mushrooms lengthwise so that they are about ¼ of an inch to 1 inch thick. Do not slice the small mushrooms.
6. Place the butter in a large skillet and heat over high heat. Add in the portabella mushrooms as well as the sage, thyme, and shallots.
7. Cook until the mushrooms have browned or for about 10 minutes.
8. While the mushroom mixture is cooking, squeeze the morels that are soaking in the broth in order to release any grit.
9. Take them out of the broth and then squeeze them once more.
10. Very carefully pour the broth into a glass container but do not pour the sediment in the container.
11. Discard the sediment.
12. If there is less than 1 ¾ cups of the soaking liquid left, add enough water to make it 1 ¾ cups.
13. Pour the broth into the skillet.
14. Clean out the bowl and place the morels back in it.
15. Squeeze the morals in order to release any grit that is left.
16. Take them out of the bowl and squeeze them again.

17. Place the morels in the skillet and discard the water.
18. Heat to a simmer.
19. While this is heating, rinse off the fennel, trim it and then discard the stalks, stems, and any bruised areas.
20. Slice the fennel thinly, then chop ¼ of a cup of the feathery part of the leaves.
21. Reserve a few of the sprigs.
22. Discard the rest.
23. Cover and chill.
24. Place the potatoes, fennel, and the turnips in your crockpot.
25. Pour the mushroom mixture into the crockpot and then add in the wine.
26. Place the lid on the crockpot and cook on low heat for 5 hours.
27. Mix the cornstarch and the whipping cream in a small bowl.
28. Turn your crockpot to high heat.
29. Add in the cornstarch slurry, the spinach, and the fennel leaves.
30. Cook for 12 minutes stirring occasionally.
31. Add salt and pepper if desired.
32. Garnish with the fennel sprigs.
33. Store and refrigerate in an airtight container.

Nutrition:
Serves: 6

- 225 calories per serving
- 7 grams of protein
- 6 grams of fat
- 38 grams of carbohydrates
- 5 grams of fiber

Chicken and Hominy Verde Stew
Ingredients:
- 2 Anaheim Chiles
- Nonstick cooking spray
- 1 ½ pounds of tomatillos
- ¼ of a cup of cilantro, chopped finely
- 1 ½ teaspoons of cumin
- 1 teaspoon of oregano
- 2 cups of chicken broth
- 2 tablespoons of EVOO
- 1 ½ cups of onion, finely chopped
- ½ of a cup of carrots, chopped
- ½ of a cup of celery chopped
- ½ of a cup of red bell pepper, chopped
- 3 tablespoons of all-purpose flour
- 4 teaspoons of garlic, chopped
- 1 pound of boneless, skinless chicken thighs, cut into bite sized pieces
- ¾ of a teaspoon of salt
- ½ of a teaspoon of black pepper
- 29 ounces of hominy, drained and rinsed
- 6 tablespoons of sour cream, reduced-fat
- Cilantro to garnish

Method:
1. Begin by preheating your broiler to high heat.
2. Cut the chilies in half, stem, and seed them.
3. Place the chilies on a baking sheet that is lined with foil, skin up.
4. Broil for about 5 minutes or until the skin is charred.
5. After they have charred place them in a paper bag, roll the top down and let them sit for 15 minutes.
6. Peel the skins off of the peppers and discard.
7. Place the tomatillos on the baking sheet and broil for about 14 minutes or until they have charred.
8. Turn them after 7 minutes.
9. Place the tomatillos, chilies, cumin, ¼ of a cup of cilantro, and the oregano in your blender as well as 1 cup of broth.
10. Blend until the mixture is smooth.
11. Place 2 teaspoons of EVOO in the bottom of a Dutch oven over medium to high heat. Make sure the bottom is completely coated.
12. Add the celery, carrots, bell pepper, and the onions to the Dutch oven.
13. Cook for 2 minutes.
14. Add in the flour, stir well and cook for another 2 minutes stirring occasionally.
15. Add the garlic to the mixture and cook for an additional minute while stirring.

16. Transfer the onion mixture to a large bowl.
17. Sprinkle your chicken with ½ of a teaspoon of salt as well as ¼ of a teaspoon of pepper.
18. Add 2 teaspoons of oil to your Dutch oven, making sure that the bottom is completely coated.
19. Add half of the chicken to the Dutch oven, cook for 3 minutes, browning all sides, add the cooked chicken to the onion mixture and repeat the process with the remaining chicken.
20. Mix the rest of the broth, the onion mixture, tomatillo mixture, and the hominy in the Dutch oven and cook on medium to high heat.
21. Bring the mixture to a boil, place the lid on the Dutch oven, reduce the heat and then cook for 45 minutes.
22. Add ½ of a teaspoon of salt as well as ¼ of a teaspoon of pepper.
23. Top with sour cream and garnish with cilantro.
24. Store and refrigerate in an airtight container.

Nutrition:
Serves: 6

- 322 calories per serving
- 14 grams of fat
- 19 grams of protein
- 31 grams of carbohydrates
- 6 grams of fiber

Chickpea Curried Stew

Ingredients:

For the pilaf

- 1 tablespoon of canola oil
- 1 cup of onion, chopped finely
- 1 cup of brown rice, not cooked
- ½ of a teaspoon of turmeric
- 3 crushed cardamom pods
- 1 cinnamon stick, 3 inches long
- 1 clove of garlic, minced
- 1 2/3 cups of water
- 1 bay leaf

For the stew

- 1 tablespoon of canola oil
- 2 cups of onions, chopped
- 1 tablespoon of ginger, grated
- 1 teaspoon of cumin
- 1 teaspoon of coriander
- ¾ of a teaspoon of turmeric
- ¼ of a teaspoon of ground red pepper
- 4 cloves of garlic, minced
- 1 cinnamon stick, 3 inches long
- 2 ½ cups of water
- 1 cup of carrots, diced
- ¼ of a teaspoon of salt
- 15 ounces of garbanzo beans drained and rinsed
- 15 ounces of fire roasted tomatoes, crushed, in their liquid
- ½ of a cup of nonfat yogurt, plain
- ¼ of a cup of cilantro, chopped

Method:

1. Begin by preparing the pilaf. Place a large skillet on the stove over medium heat.
2. Add 1 tablespoon of oil to the skillet and make sure that the bottom is completely covered.
3. Once the oil has heated, add in the onion.
4. Cook the onions for 6 minutes, stirring occasionally.
5. Next, add in the rice, turmeric, cardamom pods, cinnamon, and garlic.
6. Cook this for 1 minute stirring the entire time.
7. Next, add in the water and the bay leaf.
8. Bring the mixture to a boil.
9. Place the lid on the skillet, reduce the heat and allow to simmer for 45 minutes.

10. Allow the rice to stand for 5 minutes after it has cooked, remove the cinnamon, bay leaf, and the cardamom. Discard.
11. Next, you will prepare the stew. Place your Dutch oven on your stove top over medium to high heat.
12. Place 1 tablespoon of oil in the Dutch oven making sure that the bottom is completely coated.
13. Add in the onions and cook them for 6 minutes.
14. Next add the ginger as well as the cumin, coriander, turmeric, red pepper, garlic, and cinnamon stick.
15. Cook this for 1 minute constantly stirring it as it cooks.
16. Add in the water, carrots, chickpeas, ¼ of a teaspoon of salt, and the tomatoes.
17. Bring the mixture to a boil.
18. Place the lid on the Dutch oven, reduce the heat, and allow it to simmer for 20 minutes or until the carrots are tender.
19. Remove the cardamom and the cinnamon stick.
20. Put 1 cup of the pilaf in a bowl and top with 1 ¼ cups of the step.
21. Store and refrigerate in an airtight container.
22. Serve with 2 tablespoons of yogurt and 1 tablespoon of cilantro if desired.

Nutrition:
Serves: 4

- 431 calories per serving
- 10 grams of fat
- 12 grams of protein
- 78 grams of carbohydrates
- 10 grams of fiber

Lamb Tagine

Ingredients:
- Nonstick cooking spray
- 1 pound of boneless leg of lamb trimmed of the fat and cut into bite sized pieces
- ½ of a teaspoon of salt
- 1 ½ of a cup of onions, chopped
- 1 teaspoon of cumin
- ½ of a teaspoon of cinnamon
- ½ of a teaspoon of ground red pepper
- 6 cloves of garlic, chopped
- 2 tablespoons of honey
- 1 tablespoon of tomato paste
- ½ of a cup of dried apricots, cut into quarters
- 14 ounces of beef broth

Method:
1. Begin by coating the bottom of your Dutch oven with nonstick cooking spray and placing it over medium to high heat.
2. Sprinkle ¼ of a teaspoon of salt over the lamb.
3. Place the lamb in the pan and cook for 4 minutes or until all sides have browned.
4. Remove the lamb from the Dutch oven.
5. Place the onions in the oven and cook for 4 minutes.
6. Add in the cumin, ¼ of a teaspoon of salt, cinnamon, ground red pepper, and the garlic.
7. Cook for 1 minute, then add in the tomato paste and honey.
8. Cook for another 30 seconds stirring constantly.
9. Place the lamb back into the Dutch oven.
10. Add in the broth and the apricots.
11. Bring the mixture to a boil.
12. Place the lid on the Dutch oven and reduce the heat.
13. Cook for 1 hour.
14. Store and refrigerate in an airtight container.

Nutrition:
Serves: 4
- 386 calories per serving
- 12 grams of fat
- 42 grams of protein
- 28 grams of carbohydrates
- 4 grams of fiber

Chapter 8- 28 Day Meal Plan

In order to make meal prepping work for you, it is best to have a meal plan. In this chapter, I am going to provide you with a simple meal plan using the recipes that are in this book.

Week 1
Day 1:
Breakfast
- Peanut butter and banana overnight oats (page 25)

Lunch
- Chicken and Rainbow Veggies (page 47)

Dinner
- Lamb tagine (page 79)

Day 2:
Breakfast
- Kale and sweet potato hash (page 26)

Lunch
Sweet potato and chicken bowl (page 48)

Dinner
Chickpea curried stew (page 77)

Day 3:
Breakfast
Breakfast burrito (page 27)

Lunch
Pesto chicken Pockets (page 50)

Dinner
Pork Posole (page 72)

Day 4:
Breakfast
- Peanut butter granola bars (page --)

Lunch
- Red Pepper and Quinoa Chili (page 56)

Dinner
- Carrots and Chickpea Couscous (page 64)

Day 5:

Breakfast
- Peanut butter and banana overnight oats (page 25)

Lunch
- Greek Chicken Salad in a Jar (page 59)

Dinner
- Mushroom Bolognese (page 61)

Day 6:

Breakfast
- Breakfast Burrito page 27

Lunch
- Pesto Chicken Pockets Page 50

Dinner
- Lamb tagine Page 79

Day 7:

Breakfast
- Kale and sweet potato hash (page 26)

Lunch
- Chicken and Rainbow Veggies (page 47)

Dinner
- Root Vegetable Pot Pie (page 73)

Week 2
Day 1:
Breakfast
- Breakfast Tacos Vegan Style (page 33)

Lunch
- No Mayo Tuna Salad (page 58)

Dinner
- Carrots and chickpea couscous (page 64)

Day 2:
Breakfast
- Banana Pancakes (page 46)

Lunch
- Fiesta Chicken Bowl (page 55)

Dinner
- Lamb Tagine (page 79)

Day 3:
Breakfast
- Apricot Energy Bars (page 36)

Lunch
- Cashew Chicken and Quinoa (page 57)

Dinner
- Chickpea curried Stew (page 77)

Day 4:
Breakfast
- Avocado Egg Bowl (page 43)

Lunch
- Chicken Burrito Bowl (page 54)

Dinner
- Pot Roast and Turnip Greens (page 67)

Day 5:
Breakfast
- Blueberry Chia Seed Pudding (page 45)

Lunch
- Pesto Chicken Pocket (page 50)

Dinner
- Pasta with meat sauce (page 71)

Day 6:

Breakfast

- Blueberry Lemon Yogurt Breakfast Cake (page 39)

Lunch

- Pasta Salad in A Jar (page 60)

Dinner

- Beef Daube (page 69)

Day 7:

Breakfast

- Parfait (page 44)

Lunch

- Sweet Potato and Chicken Bowl (page 48)

Dinner

- Pulled Pork Sandwiches (page 66)

Week 3
Day 1:
Breakfast
- Breakfast Burrito (page 27)

Lunch
- Chicken and Rainbow Veggies (page 47)

Dinner
- Bourbon Peach Butter Grilled Chicken (page 63)

Day 2:
Breakfast
- Breakfast Taco Vegan Style (page 33)

Lunch
- Sweet Potato and Chicken Bowl (page 48)

Dinner-
- Carrots and Chicken Couscous (page 64)

Day 3:
Breakfast
- Banana Pancakes (page 46)

Lunch
- Chicken and Cauliflower Rice (page 51)

Dinner
- Chickpea Curried Stew (page 77)

Day 4:
Breakfast
- Avocado and Egg Bowl (page 43)

Lunch
- Red Pepper and Quinoa Chili (page 56)

Dinner
- Chicken and Hominy Verde Stew (page --)

Day 5:
Breakfast
- Breakfast Cookie (page 41)

Lunch
- Chicken and Veggie Bowl (page 55)

Dinner
- Pasta with Meat Sauce (page 71)

Day 6:

Breakfast
- Indian Baked Potato and Egg (page 38)

Lunch
- Greek Chicken Salad in a Jar (page 59)

Dinner
- Beef Daube (page 69)

Day 7:

Breakfast
- Sea Salt and Dark Chocolate Almond and Oatmeal Bake (page 40)

Lunch
- No Mayo Tuna Salad (page 58)

Dinner
- Pork Posole (page 72)

Week 4
Day 1:
Breakfast
- Egg Polenta and Refried Beans Skillet (page 37)

Lunch
- Fiesta Chicken Bowl (page 53)

Dinner
- Root Vegetable Pot Pie (page --)

Day 2:
Breakfast
- Egg Benedict Casserole (page 34)

Lunch
- Chicken and Rainbow Veggies (page 47)

Dinner
- Pulled Pork Sandwich (page 66)

Day 3:
Breakfast
- Blueberry Chia Seed Pudding (page 45)

Lunch
- Cashew chicken and Quinoa (page 57)

Dinner
- Chicken and Hominy Verde stew (page --)

Day 4:
Breakfast
- Kale and Sweet Potato (page 26)

Lunch
- Pasta salad in a jar (page 60)

Dinner
- Pot Roast and Turnip Greens (page 67)

Day 5:
Breakfast
- Parfait (page 44)

Lunch
- Pesto Chicken Pockets (page 50)

Dinner
- Carrots and Chickpea Couscous (page 64)

Day 6:
Breakfast
- Avocado and Egg Bowl (page 43)

Lunch
- Red Pepper and quinoa chili (page 56)

Dinner
- Bourbon Peach Butter Grilled Chicken (page 63)

Day 7:
Breakfast
- Breakfast cookie (page 41)

Lunch
- Sweet Potato and Chicken Bowl (page 45)

Dinner
- Mushroom Bolognese (page 61)

And there you have a 28 day make ahead meal plan using the recipes in this book.

Conclusion

Like every other good thing in life, we have now arrived at the end of this book, but the beginning of your new journey. It is in my sincerest hope that you have learned the fundamentals of meal prepping, along with some recipes that will make the new adventure easy and fun. I have tried my very best here to provide not only the simplest of recipes to make for meal prepping, but the most delicious as well.

Please remember that to reach any worthwhile goal in life requires dedication and focus. Remember why you're doing all this, have a strategic plan in place, and discipline yourself to follow through day in and day out. Once you reach the other side of your goal, you'll look back and say it was worth it.

Lastly, I'd like to once again thank you from the bottom of my heart, for choosing my book and I hope it becomes a difference maker in your life.

Sincerely,
Dorothy Hoffman

Made in the USA
Middletown, DE
11 December 2017